WALKAROUND
MODEL RAILROAD
Track Plans — WITHDRAWN

MODEL RAILROAD HANDBOOK NO. 29

BY DON MITCHELL

EDITOR: Michael Emmerich
ASSISTANT EDITOR: Marcia Stern
ART DIRECTOR: Lawrence Luser
STAFF ARTISTS: Mark Watson, Phil Kirchmeier,
Robert Wegner, Steve Davis, Glenda Oslage, Lisa Bergman

 KALMBACH BOOKS.

First printing, 1991. Second printing, 1992.

Easy access to all points on a layout just makes sense, and that's what a walkaround design provides, as this layout under construction illustrates.

INTRODUCTION

Model railroads are always built by people, so they should always be built for people

Designing your dream layout requires consideration of many factors. The maxim above expresses my belief that the most important factor is the human element. Inclusion of the people considerations illustrated by the plans in this book will pay big dividends in the future enjoyment of your layout.

The most important of these people considerations is access — so much so that the first three rules of layout design are all offshoots of access.

The first rule is for access during construction. This is so easy to achieve (just move around the benchwork) that most model railroaders don't even consider it. Yet construction access is important. The best model railroads are

created when the layout room is prepared before benchwork is started. Such projects as installing wiring for layout lighting, finishing the ceiling, installing valances and lighting fixtures, and painting the backdrop are more easily accomplished when access to these areas is unhindered.

The second rule is for access during operation. Most of us give consideration to how we're going to run our trains. The best operation occurs when trackwork is directly accessible by aisles leading from the entryway. This layout arrangement is usually referred to as a "walkaround," and is the basis for the layouts in this book.

The third rule is for access during maintenance, and this probably has been the least considered factor in model railroad design. Almost everything that

moves on a model railroad — and that includes track shifts caused by changes in temperature or humidity — will need maintenance. Murphy's Law dictates that the first layout component to require major maintenance will be the most inaccessible, such as a turnout buried 3″ from the wall, 3″ below an upper track, or 3″ under a cherished scenic feature. Achieving good access to all parts of a layout is usually worth the sacrifices involved, even if it means eliminating some trackwork.

WALKAROUND DESIGN

Although good access is the primary advantage of walkaround design, there are others. Combining walkaround control with walkaround design permits the operator to see (and hear) the condition of the train and track. If the operator is

HEIGHT RELATIONSHIPS*

Height (A)	Ratio (B)	Remarks (C)
92"	2H/R	High reach without strain. Top of layout or wall storage.
74"	H	Height. Top of center backdrops for no-see-over viewing.
69½"	H-4½	Eye level.
57"	$2H/R^2$	Underarm height. Top of manual controls.
48"	H/R	Elbow height. Good choice for layout (track) height.
35"	$2H/R^3$	Resting hand height. Low layout height; 3 inches higher preferable to allow for bent elbow position.
22"	$2H/R^4$	Knee height. Good height for low storage shelves and electrical outlets.
18"	H/R^3	Seat height/ Coffee table height for a model railroad.

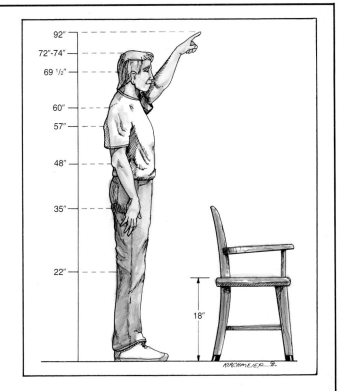

(*) Adapted from "Humanscale" (a series of manuals published by the MIT Press, 1974) by Nils Differient, Alvin R. Tilley, David Harman, and Joan C. Bardaguy.

(A) Suggested modern day practice based on an assumed height of 74". This height has been selected to accommodate all but 2-3 percent of the U.S. male population.

(B) These ratios are derived from the Golden Section of Pythagoras and were used in selecting proportions for architectural components of that early era. H = height of the person and R = 1.62. Substituting you height for H gives a basis for customizing layout height to your own proportions, but consider the height of likely visitors, too.

(C) The remarks indicate model railroad adaptations for ancient usages leaving no excuse for saying "It's all Greek to me."

---

where the train is, turnouts can be thrown by hand. Some turnouts are better operated electrically; still, an on-scene operator can readily verify that turnouts are set for the correct route. And with the operator able to accompany the train, it's not necessary to build signal systems to show what the train is doing when it is out of sight from a central operating location.

Another advantage is that if trouble arises, the operator is right there to detect the problem and take immediate corrective action. Derailments, running onto the wrong track, and stalled trains are examples of such problems.

A more abstract advantage to walkaround control is the closeness of feeling between the operator and the train. The scenery and the train are right at hand rather than being viewed from afar. The change of perspective enjoyed by the walkaround operator can be rewarding in itself.

Walkaround design has few disadvantages. More space has to be allotted for aisles, the track plan has to be configured so that the trains move along the aisles near the operator, and the operator can't always remain in one location while trains run. Considering what can

be accomplished with walkaround layout design, these seem a small price to pay for the many advantages.

DESIGNING FOR PEOPLE

Including people considerations in design goes back to ancient times (see the table). The art has progressed far enough to be given its own name, "ergonomics." Present-day ergonomic applications range from the exotic, such as space shuttles, to the commonplace, such as kitchen arrangements. Applied to model railroad design, ergonomics allows classification of all layouts into just two components: those sections where everything from backdrop to aisle edge is within easy reach for operation and maintenance; and all others.

DESIGNS WITHIN REACH

On most of the layouts in this book the effective reach from an aisle to the rear of the top surface is 30″. There's more to that 30″ width than meets the eye, however. Easy reach depends on the vertical relationships between the layout and the modeler, and on the purpose of the reach. As the layout gets higher with respect to the modeler, the

effective reach becomes shorter. Effective reach also becomes shorter as the purpose of the reach becomes more complicated: It's more difficult to spike down rail than to lift a car off the track.

Where the layout surface is high, reach can be extended by providing a stool or other elevated base to stand on. More complicated work can be done further into the layout when there is a surface to lean on. More space, however, must be provided behind the modeler when it's necessary to bend over to work on the layout. Consideration also has to be given to what's above and below access spaces, particularly in areas of multilevel trackwork.

The most frequently encountered out-of-reach situation occurs when the track is turned back on itself for 180 degrees or more. When such turnback curves are used to achieve the best model railroad, every trick and technique in the designer's book should be used to place the maximum amount of layout within easy reach. A simple solution is to use short radius curves such as those on the Oakville Central — an example of examining access and reach from the ground up.

THE OAKVILLE CENTRAL

A small HO layout that's interesting to operate

While visions of full basements may dance in our heads, the realities of modern life often dictate that our model railroads be fitted into much smaller areas. The area available for the Oakville Central was but 3'1" x 5'10" — the dimensions of a trundle bed drawer designed to slide out from under a regular bed. Not only was the area restricted but also the vertical clearance was limited to 2" or 3" by a requirement that the layout fit on top of the trundle bed mattress. Flat terrain was obviously indicated.

Despite the cramped conditions, it was still possible to get some interesting operation worked in if 15"-radius curves were used. Looking at the plan which evolved, it's easy to see that the emphasis was placed on switching cars to and from various industries. A continuous route was also included for those times when just plain running trains is the order of the day.

Some comments about layout design planning are pertinent to the task of trying to achieve a reasonable operation in a small space. Clearances between track and structures have to be plotted to closer tolerances than for larger layouts, as there is less room for adjusting things by eye during the actual construction. Double-line drawings give a better feel for the width of the track than do single-line drawings. Either method is acceptable as long as proper clearances are maintained on both sides of the track. Templates are handy to use when drawing plans for small areas, especially when sectional track components are to be used.

Critical trackwork should be located first, as it will determine the location of the rest of the track. The two end curves and the passing track/crossing area turned out to be the critical locations on the Oakville Central. There are no hard and fast rules for determining what will be critical; look first at tracks near the edges of the layout and at areas where there are a lot of turnouts in proximity to each other. Be prepared to do a fair amount of trial and error fitting before things fall into place. Of course, there should be some sort of rough sketch made of the layout idea before detailed planning is started.

When working in small areas, track and structures have to be located concurrently unless the buildings are going to be scratchbuilt or kitbashed to fit. Templates for structures were prepared to the same scale as the track templates, using dimensions listed in the Walthers catalog. Track positions were shifted and alternate structures were fitted until a workable scheme developed.

Clearances were plotted to allow 1½" between the track center line and buildings on curves, and 1" on straight track. These figures were interpolated from NMRA Standards and Recommended Practices based on the 15" radius used and the type of equipment to be operated.

Short cars, short locomotives, and shortline operation are what the Oakville Central is all about. Freight cars should be selected from the many 40- and 50-foot types available. Shorter cars will obviously make things easier; longer cars should be avoided, as they tend to create all sorts of problems on the short-radius curves. Locomotives should

Al Kalbfleisch photo.

Like the Oakville Central, industries, big and small, with rail service are one of the characteristics of Don Cleke's Wicasset & Maine railroad.

Layout at a glance

Name: OAKVILLE CENTRAL
Scale: HO
Space: 3'1" x 5'10" x 3"
Location: Under bed
Operation: Switching oval
Emphasis: Small radius curves

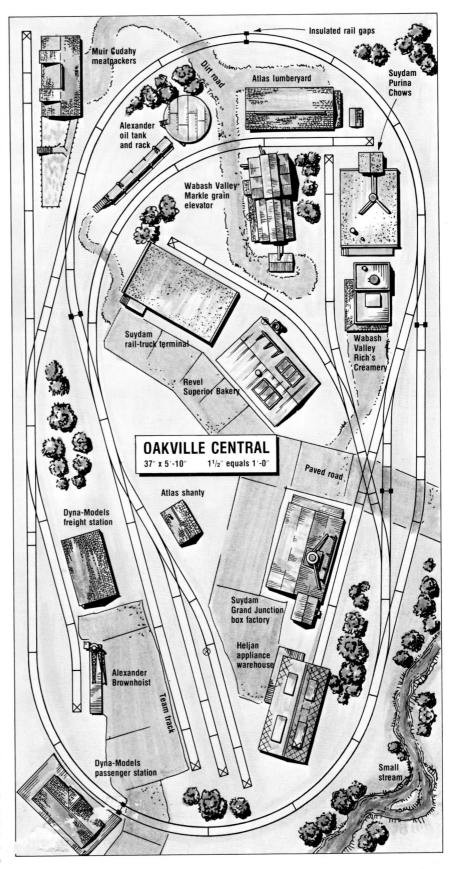

be similarly restricted in length. Steam locomotives should have a short wheelbase, which means four driving wheels or some very small six-driver locomotives. Diesels should be limited to B-B types or industrial locomotives meeting the same criteria as the steam engines. A low-budget short line, particularly one that is involved mostly in local switching operations, would probably operate without a caboose to its name.

One or two locomotives could be used to handle the Oakville Central's business. The insulating gaps depicted provide plenty of flexibility for simultaneous operation of two trains. Note that the spur to the lumber company could be used as a lead for switching the yard in complete independence of any operation on the main line.

Some form of car order system should be used as a basis for directing car movements. Several of these systems have been described in past issues of MODEL RAILROADER. A more readily obtainable description of car movement systems is contained in the book HOW TO OPERATE YOUR MODEL RAILROAD by Bruce Chubb. Any car order system will add interest to operation on the Oakville Central by giving some purpose to the switching movements. The problems that occur in sorting out the cars add enjoyment much like solving crossword or jigsaw puzzles.

Switching movements mean that the cars will have to be uncoupled from each other frequently. Use of uncoupling ramps would be difficult, at best, because of the many uncoupling locations and the sharp curves being used. Uncoupling tools can be made or purchased to assist in this task.

In line with the theme that the Oakville Central is designed for operation, all of the buildings represent industries which have rail service. Available real estate is at too much of a premium to have houses or similar nonrailroad structures taking up space. The existence of nonrailroad buildings is suggested by the roads leading off the edges of the railroad baseboard.

Selection of the structures was based on several premises. Industries served by rail have been mentioned. A mixture of plastic, cardstock, and wood construction was chosen to provide a variety of modelbuilding interest. As templates were essential to the design

process, only structures with known dimensions were included. (It's too bad that model manufacturers don't print dimensions on the outside of their packages.) Low- and mid-price range kits were specified to minimize costs. The resulting buildings had to be fairly

sturdy, as they will undergo frequent handling. The restricted vertical clearance means that all buildings and rolling stock have to be removed before the layout drawer is rolled back into the stored position. The Oakville Central is truly a low-overhead operation.

An impressive array of trackwork leads to State Belt Railway's enginehouse on the San Francisco waterfront. Retired for the day are two 1000-horsepower Alco switchers.

BEKIN UNITED RR

A small HO switching pike that proves big isn't always better

Maybe right now you don't have the space, time, or even the inclination to build that basement-size dream layout. Still, you'd like to get up out of that armchair and build something. Well, never fear, there's always the switching layout, and it doesn't have to be something "second best." In fact, a small switching pike like this HO scale Bekin United RR (BURR) can offer plenty of operating pleasure.

It can look more realistic, too, because we can forgo the sharp-radius curves necessary on small table-type continuous-run layouts. The curves are larger, and instead of watching trains go round and round we can focus on switching movements. There's a yard with an engine terminal, a waterfront industrial district, and a short stretch of main line for conjuring up dreams of greater things.

Switching requires a lot of reaching to couple and uncouple cars, so the yard and industries have been located in front of the main line to provide the best possible operating access. This also simplifies maintenance, as it puts the switches up front where you can get at them.

The only potential maintenance problem foreseen is that the double-slip switch on the main line might be a little far away for fine soldering if it can't be reached from the back side. Even if you're handlaying the track, consider using commercially manufactured switches at such locations. If worst comes to worst, such switches can be removed as a unit for repair or replacement.

DESIGN PARAMETERS

The design of the BURR appears straightforward, but there's more here than meets the eye. The modeler for whom I designed it wanted it to be sturdy enough to withstand the rigors of frequent moving, yet small enough to fit in the spaces likely to be available. It had to be large enough to provide a high degree of operating interest by itself, yet have the potential for expanding into a permanent layout or hooking up with a group's modular layout.

The size was based on my experience with a similar movable layout of my own. Since there was no way of knowing the exact dimensions of future locations for that layout, measurements were made at several houses and then the following were selected as typical:

- Door: 30" wide, 78" high
- Hall: 36" wide
- Spare room: 9' x 11' x 8' high

Taking these as limits, any movable layout section should be no wider than 30" if we want to move it through a doorway while holding it flat. This 30" limit is also a reasonable width for access to all parts of the layout when it is placed against a wall.

The maximum length of a layout section is dictated by doorways, halls, and the room where the layout will be set up. An 8' length is the maximum that can be handled around a corner and through a doorway. When we butt one 8' table against the end of another (as on the BURR), the length grows to 10'-6". This fits nicely into our 9' x 11' minimum-size room.

The remaining size consideration is the vertical depth of the benchwork sections. If the sections are 30" wide and 8' long, then 12" is the maximum thickness for the framework plus permanent scenery. If the 12" thickness is too limiting, you can shorten the benchwork length to 72". Then the sections can be stood on end and moved through doorways, permitting the thickness to be increased to 28". The shorter 6' sections also permit the layout to be set up in a 6' x 9' room.

TRACK DESIGN

Sidings on the BURR had to be able to accommodate trains 8' long. Since this is the length of each benchwork section, the yard and its switching lead have to be on separate sections. Even so, longer trains will have to be split between two or more yard tracks.

An industrial area was added to the yard lead section. A short runaround here allows a car to be placed on the cor-

Freight house

2.3

0

2

Water

Enginehouse

Sand

Coal

Ashes

.5

Warehouse   Industrial area   Wharf

30 r

30 r

24" r

30 r

Team track

Station

1   1

Layout at a glance

Name: BEKIN UNITED RR
Scale: HO
Space: Two 8' x 2' 6" x 1' sections
Location: Movable
Operation: Switching
Emphasis: Fitting average spare room

Plan scale in feet

1   6"   0   1   2   3

Turnouts

No. 4   No. 6   No. 6 double-slip

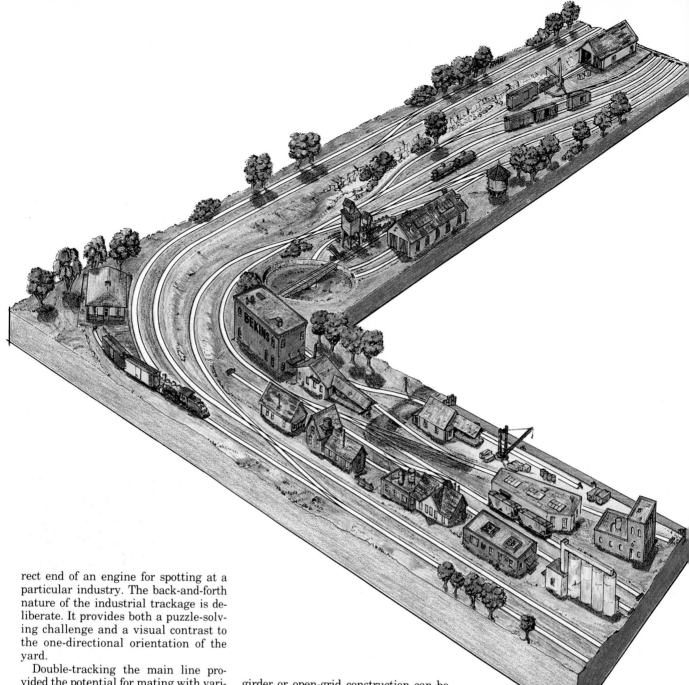

rect end of an engine for spotting at a particular industry. The back-and-forth nature of the industrial trackage is deliberate. It provides both a puzzle-solving challenge and a visual contrast to the one-directional orientation of the yard.

Double-tracking the main line provided the potential for mating with various types of modules. The combination of 3″ track spacing and 30″ radius provides adequate clearance for the long engines and cars. The trackwork at section ends can be easily rebuilt when necessary to adapt the BURR to a specific modular layout standard.

If modular group hookup isn't a strong consideration, the same amount of operation could be accomplished on a single-track main line with a passing siding. For the BURR this would mean removing the inner mainline tracks between the section ends and the crossover switches, which could also be removed. This would simplify building and maintaining the BURR and eliminate the mainline double-slip switch.

CONSTRUCTION SUGGESTIONS

Movable layout sections should be constructed from strong light materials that are easy to work with. Either L-girder or open-grid construction can be used, but grid is preferable where layout thickness is a concern. Linn Westcott's book *How to Build Model Railroad Benchwork* (Kalmbach Publishing Co.) covers both methods.

The legs should be easily detachable for moves. Bolts, washers, and wing nuts work well. If you plan on taking the layout down and putting it up a lot, consider hinging the legs so they will fold up into the layout. Adding adjustable screw feet to the legs for leveling is a good idea, particularly when mating these sections with others in a modular layout.

Many suitable scenery techniques are available, but most are based on the use of plaster in one form or another. Plaster scenery can grow surprisingly heavy, though, so if frequent moves are anticipated, consider using the structural foam techniques described by Malcolm Furlow in his book,

HO Narrow Gauge Railroad You Can Build (Kalmbach).

To join layout sections you can use C-clamps, specific modular techniques, or simply drill holes through the adjoining framing and install bolts. Joining the tracks is an equally simple matter. Carry the roadbed right to the joint, but cut the track off 2″ or 3″ short of the joint. Use short pieces of rail (or standard lengths of sectional track) to close the gap. Rail joiners are all that's needed to hold these joiner track sections in place.

Designing a layout to be accessible, movable, and full of operation can bring a lot of long-lasting fun into model railroading. Movable design belies the old adage "You can't take it with you when you go."

Photo by George A. Forero Jr.

A Manufacturers Railway Alco S2 switches at St Louis, Missouri, on a blistering July day.

Photo by Jim Shaughnessy

This switcher, a 44-ton diesel-electric Union Freight GE, lumbers down Atlantic Avenue in Boston.

UNION PACIFIC

Beating the problem of too little space with a multiple-tiered layout

The economic pressures that have caused the railroad industry to change have also affected model railroaders. Emulating today's prototypes, which have become bigger and longer, has become even more challenging because the high cost of housing has made obtaining ample layout space increasingly difficult. Thus, layout builders are opting for alternatives less grand than modeling the modern Union Pacific.

Yet, that need not be. You can usually find enough space to accommodate the modeling of a modern railroad. There are two keys. The first is recognizing the difference between area and space. Area (i.e., 4' x 8') is the way we have thought about our model railroads since the inception of the hobby. Space, however, is what we actually use. In reality no model railroad can exist without extending into the third dimension. Model railroads have only recently begun to exploit all available layout space — roughly corresponding with the changes in prototype equipment and operation. John Al-len's floor-to-ceiling scenery on his Gorre & Daphetid was one early example in the modeling field; John Armstrong's multilevel layout plans were another.

The second key is to analyze objectively some of our social conventions about housing. The space in most of our homes has been partitioned into single-purpose rooms. How much of the space in these rooms is used? Not as much as you might think. If you look at any room, you'll see that about 20 percent of it is always unused: the space in the 16" between the ceiling (normally 96" high) and the tops of doors and windows (80" high).

Above-the-doorway layouts have been built, but they're not common. Plans for a few appeared in MODEL RAILROAD-ER Magazine back in the late 1940s and early 1950s, when homes were smaller and space restrictions precluded single-purpose layout rooms. The Union Pacific (UP) track design blends this old idea with modern concepts of space utilization and accessibility to create a sizable layout in a modest-sized multipurpose room.

FROM THE TOP DOWN

The top level of the UP is a walk-under layout that can be fitted into the above-the-doorway space of an 8' x 9' room. The track arrangement is basically a twice-around continuous oval. A wye connection to a descending helix allows operation of the top level as a reversing loop.

A high-level layout introduces considerations not encountered in conventional model railroading. The "up" location for all top-level trackwork means that it will be viewed at both an angle and at a distance that precludes close inspection. With no need for detailed appearance, common sectional and flex track components can be used, which, of course, provide construction and maintenance advantages. In fact, this is an instance where turnouts with integral top-mounted switch machines would be more desirable than other types.

The viewing angle also means that the undersides of cars and locomotives will be more noticeable. Painting such elements as bright metal axles, bottom surfaces, and even the near sides of the rails will help prevent jarring false notes in the overall appearance of the railroad.

The station area trackwork cutting diagonally across the room is supported by the helix, while the track along the wall is supported by brackets. Many commercial shelf-bracket systems are available for mounting these sections. Spacing and mounting details depend on the particular system used, but two general principles apply. First, the brackets should be fastened to the house framing studs, not just to the wallboard. Second, the roadbed and scenery should be kept as light as possible.

The top-level trackwork can be simplified a bit. Assuming the layout will be extended downward, turnouts A and B can be eliminated at the cost of removing continuous run capability. Turnouts C and D form a lap-siding connection that increases the flexibility and capacity of the station passing tracks. Removing these turnouts converts the station trackage into a conventional passing siding.

John C. Illman photo

Two Union Pacific SD60s and a C30-7 crest the summit of the Blue Mountains in Oregon. Such a setting, with rises in elevation, is perfect for a multiple-tiered layout.

TURNOUT DATA

Linn Westcott, late editor of MODEL RAILROADER, developed the following data by converting prototype turnout dimensions from the American Railroad Engineering Association (AREA) to HO (1/87) scale:

Switch number	Frog angle	Average radius	Minimum radius	Ladder spacing	Fanout spacing
8	7.15°	83.2"	67.2"	14.4"	10.4"
7	8.17°	63.7"	49.9"	12.6"	9.1"
6	9.53°	46.8"	35.0"	10.8"	7.8"
5	11.42°	32.5"	24.1"	9.0"	6.5"
4.5	12.68°	26.3"	19.3"	8.1"	5.5"
4	14.25°	20.8"	16.8"	7.2"	5.2"
36"r	10.86°	36.0"	36.0"	9.6"	6.8"
30"r	11.88°	30.0"	30.0"	8.7"	6.2"
24"r	13.28°	24.0"	24.0"	7.8"	5.6"

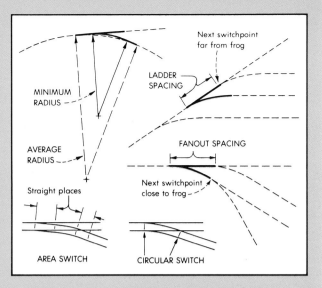

- Switch number is the usual identification method for model railroad turnouts.
- Frog angle indicates the amount of divergence between the intersecting rails in a turnout.
- Average radius is the minimum radius circular curve in which the indicated turnout will fit with a perfect match at each end.
- Minimum radius is the radius of the curved leg of the turnout between the points and the frog.
- Ladder spacing is the distance between the straight track portions of two turnouts for yard tracks to have a spacing of 13 scale feet (1.8" in HO) when led off the curved portions of the turnouts. A crossover would require twice the ladder spacing.
- Fanout spacing is the minimum distance between two consecutive turnouts, but be careful that parallel tracks leading from such an arrangement are not too closely spaced.

Turnout numbers 4.5 or 5 are usually compatible with other minimum radii on the layout. The minimum radius through the curved portion of these straight-frog turnouts may mean, however, that some long-wheelbase steam locomotives will require modification to work reliably. Because turnouts larger than number 5 are not usually needed for compatibility with other layout radii, appearance becomes the determining factor in choosing which size, if any, to use.

THE TERMINAL LEVEL

More under-utilized space is found on the walls of a conventional room. Replacing pictures, plants, and other decorative paraphernalia with shelf and modular layout components can add length and breadth to a model railroad such as the UP. The space equivalent of a conventional layout is gained by vertically stacking multiple shelves. The illustration on page 13 shows how a passenger station, freight yard, and small engine terminal can be added while preserving walk-in access.

Mating modern UP equipment with a modest layout space must be performed carefully to ensure successful train operation. The helix is drawn as a 24"-radius circle, but it should be constructed as a slightly egg-shaped combination of Atlas Custom line No. 4 turnouts and 22"-radius curves. The Atlas turnouts are recommended because they have a No. 4.5 frog (see the table), more compatible with long rolling stock.

The most critical track is the wye connection between turnout "E" and the passenger arrival track. The reverse curve in this area will determine the length of passenger cars that can be operated successfully. The effect of the reverse curve can be minimized by using constant radius turnouts for the wye connections and rearranging the reverse curves so the straight section between them is as long as possible.

The passenger trackage is arranged so that all backing movements while turning trains are made downhill. The movements involved are: (1) backing downhill from the arrival track through the wye connection to the helix turnout "E," then (2) moving clockwise up the helix past the other wye connection, and (3) backing downhill into the departure track.

The freight yard is designed to be worked by a switch engine pulling cuts of cars uphill (clockwise) out of the yard onto the helix, and then pushing them downhill back into the yard. The engine terminal is connected to the helix uphill from the freight yard so that it can be used as a switcher pocket. The level track alongside the enginehouse can also be used as a yard lead if it isn't being used for locomotive storage.

You can use long trailer flats and passenger cars in such tight quarters, but exercise care in preparing track and equipment. Rails have to be checked for correct gauge and carefully aligned in both the horizontal and vertical planes. Equipment has to be properly weighted, wheels checked and gauged, bolster pivots checked for horizontal and vertical motion, and couplers adjusted or modified for wide swing.

If all this sounds as though it's too much effort, the UP can still be modeled by backdating everything to the era of 40' and 50' cars. Some of the larger steam engines of that era have been available in ready-to-run versions capable of operating on the radii shown. The trailer-train theme can be preserved by using shorter flatcars capable of holding only one trailer, or the entire yard can be reoriented by replacing the trailer facilities with railroad-served industries like warehouses and icing plants.

THE LIVING LEVEL

In keeping with the UP's non-conventional design, a sleeping arrangement has been included in the plan for the living level. To further stimulate thought about multi-purpose use of available space, a removable 2' x 4' module has been included to show how one of these units could be connected to the more permanently fixed home layout.

A table and dresser would fit in the room, too. The mining scene above the dresser shows a two-level industrial alternative to the engine terminal.

The tri-base arrangement for supporting the helix allows the bed to be swung out into the room, providing somewhat easier access for housekeeping and to the inside of the helix. The dimensions are not critical. More room for housekeeping chores can be created by raising the living level track.

CORKSCREW CONSTRUCTION

The crucial element in combining conventional layout practices with increased space utilization is the helix. Spiraling trains up and down between levels may require a non-conventional outlook toward model railroad operation, but helixes have been built and used successfully. Although they only take up the space equivalent of a small

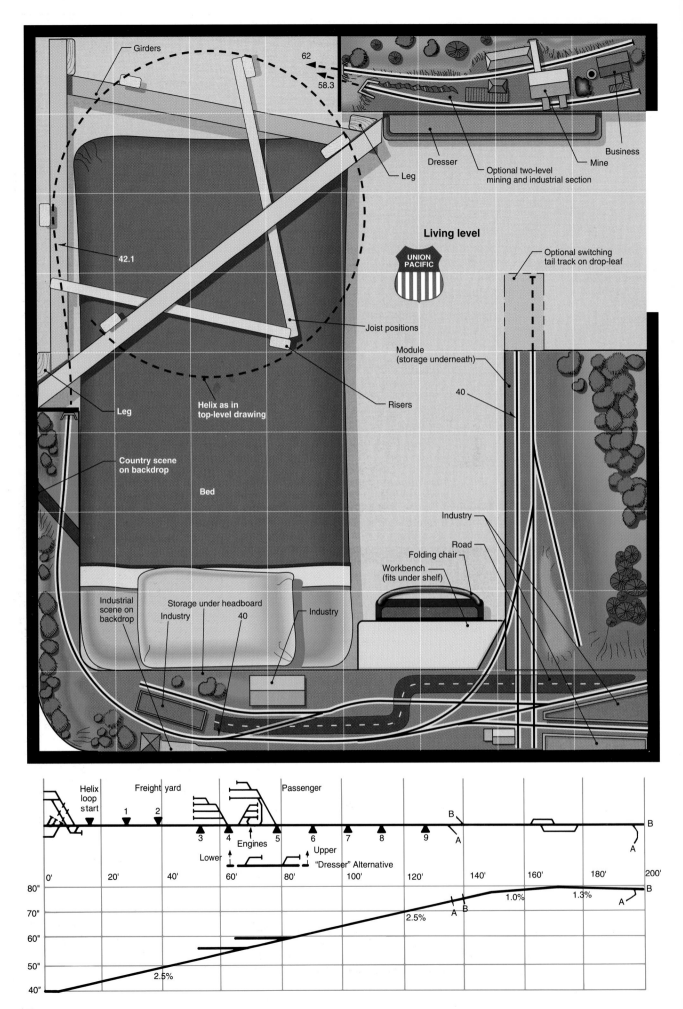

Girders

62

58.3

Dresser

Optional two-level
mining and industrial section

Mine

Business

Leg

42.1

Living level

UNION
PACIFIC

Optional switching
tail track on drop-leaf

Joist positions

Module
(storage underneath)

Leg

40

Helix as in
top-level drawing

Risers

**Country scene
on backdrop**

Bed

Industry

Road

Folding chair

Workbench
(fits under shelf)

Industrial
scene on
backdrop
Industry

Storage under headboard
40

Industry

Helix
loop
start

Freight yard

Passenger

1   2

3   4   5   6   7   8   9

Engines

B

A

B

A

Lower

Upper
"Dresser" Alternative

0'   20'   40'   60'   80'   100'   120'   140'   160'   180'   200'

80"

70"

1.0%   1.3%

B

60"

2.5%

A   B

A

50"

2.5%

40"

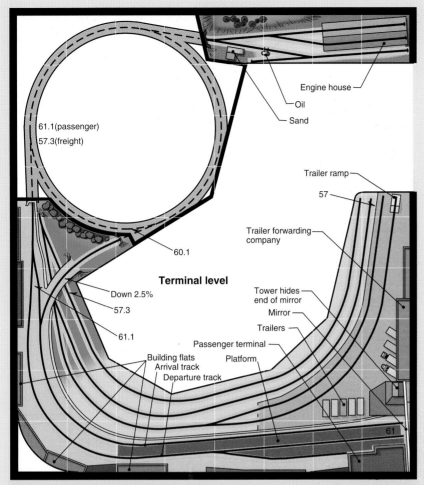

Engine house
Oil
Sand

61.1(passenger)
57.3(freight)

60.1

Terminal level

Down 2.5%
57.3
61.1

Building flats
Arrival track
Departure track

Trailer ramp
57

Trailer forwarding
company

Tower hides
end of mirror
Mirror
Trailers
Passenger terminal
Platform

61

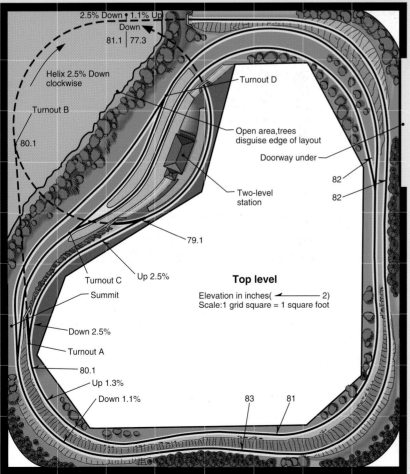

2.5% Down   1.1% Up
Down
81.1 | 77.3

Helix 2.5% Down
clockwise

Turnout B

80.1

Turnout C   Up 2.5%

Summit

Down 2.5%

Turnout A

80.1

Up 1.3%

Down 1.1%

Turnout D

Open area, trees
disguise edge of layout

Doorway under
82
82

Two-level
station

79.1

Top level

Elevation in inches(◄————— 2)
Scale:1 grid square = 1 square foot

83   81

closet, don't underestimate the amount of railroad you get with a helix. The 10 + loops used for the UP provide 125' of running track! This is a much larger model railroad than it appears at first glance.

Chapter 7 of Linn Westcott's book HOW TO BUILD MODEL RAILROAD BENCHWORK (Kalmbach, 1979) includes an excellent discussion on supporting a helical spiral. Use of his notched riser and laminated thin roadbed technique would allow the UP helix to be constructed with only a 2.5 percent grade to gain adequate clearance between each level.

The UP helix is too large to fit through a normal doorway in one piece. If it has to be moved in or out, *don't* cut it into two 180-degree sections. Only three cuts are needed in the helix roadbed: at the joint with the top level, at the bottom joint with the living level, and at the middle of the helix. Cut through the notched risers on the level adjacent to the middle cut, then turn the two resulting helix sections on their sides and carry them through the door like huge wheels of cheese. Reassembly requires only a few splice plates.

A UNIVERSAL PLAN?

The endless design possibilities of connecting a helix to multiple shelves make the Union Pacific layout idea almost a Universal Plan for model railroads. The space utilization ideas of the UP, however non-conventional, are more important than specific track arrangement.

The UP can be fitted into an even smaller space by reducing the minimum radius. The inside of the helix should remain at least 20″ in diameter, however, and the center access aisle should be at least 3′ wide to stay reasonably comfortable. At that size, operation of the UP by more than one person had better involve only close friends.

The UP design encourages you to experiment. It challenges you to be innovative. And to model railroaders who still bemoan their lack of layout space, pay heed to this modification of Horace Greeley's renowned advice: "Go UP, young man!"

Large locomotives epitomize the Union Pacific, and if think you don't have enough space to build a layout that would permit realistic operation of these giants, think again. This track plan shows how you can run large Union Pacific locomotives on even a small layout.

ANGELS BRANCH

Helixes and small-radius curves enhance a wonderful HO prototype layout

If you find the concept of mating helixes with small layout spaces charming then you should find the prospect of matching such an arrangement with a perfect prototype irresistible. Rick Mugele, working on his own, came up with an exquisite combination of helixes and small-radius curves to match a jewel-like prototype with an 8' x 9' space.

THE LAYOUT PLAN

The Angels Branch of the Sierra Ry. operated from September 1902 to March 1939. Departing the Sierra's main line at Jamestown, California, it ran to the fabled Gold Rush town of Angels Camp, a site forever chiseled into history by Mark Twains's celebrated jumping frog.

Set on the western slope of the High Sierras, the Angels Branch crossed the rugged canyon of the Stanislaus River using 4.15 percent grades, 28-degree curves, and four switchbacks. Toss in a good-size bridge, 40-lb. rail, and lots of trestles, cuts, and fills, and here's a line that makes an almost perfect prototype for a model railroad.

Rick's three-deck arrangement for his HO Angels Branch gives a sense of the real operation and scenery. The route from Jamestown down to the Stanislaus River bridge and back up to Angels Camp yields a run of 3½ scale miles full of slow curves, steep grades, and switchbacks.

The separate decks break the run into a series of dioramas, an effective way of creating the impression of a large scene in a small area. Spreading the focal points of railroad activity around the room forces the viewer to look at only one scene at a time.

Look at Jamestown, for instance. Angels Camp is behind you while McArdle's switch is below and out of your line of sight. With the structures, scenery, lighting, and backdrop adjusted to enhance this "window" effect, an illusion of depth and space is created that belies the physical dimensions of the layout space.

RIDING THE BRANCH

Starting at Jamestown, on the top deck, the layout skips the prototype's climb over Table Mountain and starts down the canyon (top helix) right outside town.

Arriving at the middle deck the line passes through scenes representing both sides of the Stanislaus River. On the down (northbound) trip, the scenes would be those on the south side of the river: Tuttletown, Mormon Gulch, Jeffersonville, and Table Mountain. This is almost the reverse of the prototype sequence, but that's one of the compromises necessary to match the track elevations with effective scenic illusions.

The line then descends the lower helix to the bottom deck, which depicts the crossing of the Stanislaus River. The real Melones area was almost a full-size diorama, with the canyon walls forcing the railroad to weave back and forth along the edges of the scene. The mining complex in the canyon was surrounded by trackage on three sides, and included mine and mill structures, a small town, and a 3'-gauge mine tram. The mills were powered by a large water flume which entered a pipeline before crossing under the railroad near the river bridge.

From the bottom deck, the model line runs back up through the middle deck, which this time represents Carson Hill and the Greenstone Spur on the north side of the river. From there it climbs up to the branch terminus at Angels Camp on the top deck. The cross-section view shows the entire arrangement.

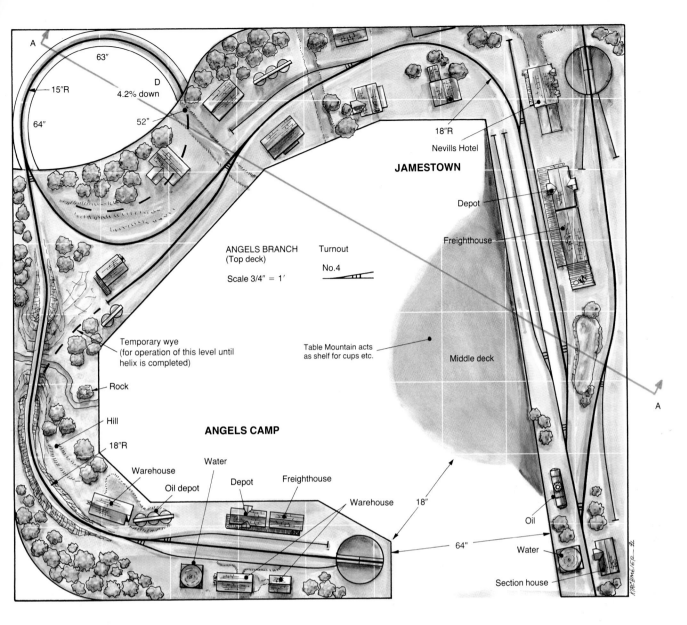

A
63"
15"R
D
4.2% down
64"
52"

ANGELS BRANCH
(Top deck)

Turnout

No.4

Scale 3/4" = 1'

18"R

Nevills Hotel

JAMESTOWN

Depot

Freighthouse

Temporary wye
(for operation of this level until
helix is completed)

Table Mountain acts
as shelf for cups etc.

Middle deck

Rock

Hill

18"R

ANGELS CAMP

A

Water

Warehouse

Depot

Freighthouse

Oil depot

Warehouse

18"

Oil

64"

Water

Section house

Layout at a glance

Name: ANGELS BRANCH
Scale: HO
Space: 8' x 9' x 8'
Location: Small room
Operation: Small branch line
Emphasis: Prototypic small radii

A typical Angels Camp train crosses the Tuttletown Trestle. This is as long as these branch line trains got because of the steep terrain and switchbacks that could accommodate nothing longer. Model Die Casting's Old-timer shorty passenger cars are dead ringers for those used on the line.

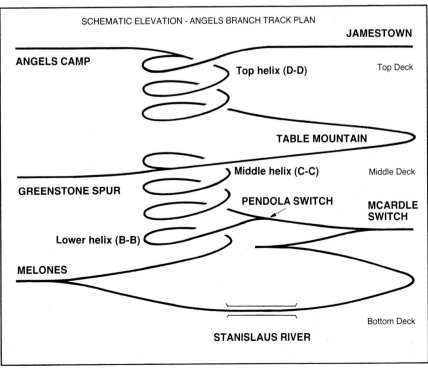

SCHEMATIC ELEVATION - ANGELS BRANCH TRACK PLAN

JAMESTOWN

ANGELS CAMP

Top helix (D-D)

Top Deck

TABLE MOUNTAIN

Middle helix (C-C)

Middle Deck

GREENSTONE SPUR

PENDOLA SWITCH

MCARDLE
SWITCH

Lower helix (B-B)

MELONES

Bottom Deck

STANISLAUS RIVER

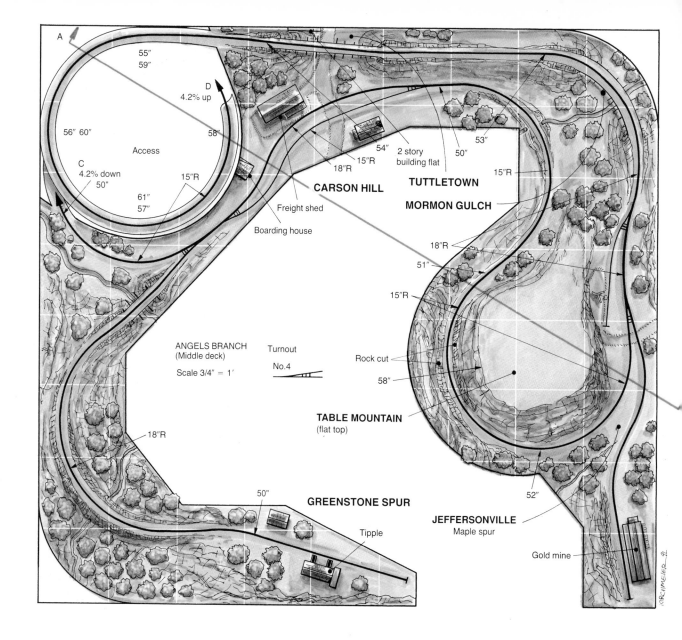

55"
59"

56" 60"

D
4.2% up

Access

58"

C
4.2% down
50"

61"
57"

15"R

A

CARSON HILL

Freight shed

Boarding house

54"
18"R

15"R

2 story
building flat

TUTTLETOWN

MORMON GULCH

53"

50"

18"R

51"

15"R

15"R

18"R

58"

ANGELS BRANCH
(Middle deck)

Scale 3/4" = 1'

Turnout

No.4

Rock cut

TABLE MOUNTAIN
(flat top)

18"R

50"

GREENSTONE SPUR

Tipple

52"

JEFFERSONVILLE
Maple spur

Gold mine

OPERATION

The layout is designed for point-to-point operation between Jamestown and Angels Camp, with the tracks on the middle deck and the helixes used twice during the run, once going down and again coming back up, as shown in the schematic elevation.

The lower deck is actually a reversing loop, but this is disguised by the switchbacks. The correct sequence for running this loop depends on the timetable direction of the train. Northbound out of Jamestown, trains continue forward off the lower helix into the switchback at McArdle. From there they head over the Stanislaus River bridge into Melones. They leave Melones by backing uphill to Pendola, where they reverse direction and head up the helix toward Angels Camp.

Several industries and station stops along the route add operating interest. Remember, though, that the middle deck represents two different sections of railroad. Switching at Table Mountain and Jeffersonville is done by trains on the south (Jamestown) side of the river, while Carson Hill and Greenstone Spur are worked on the north (Angels Camp) side. An ancillary operation could be added by converting the Melones tramway to N gauge and using HO bodies on N scale mechanisms and trucks, a combination called HOn2½.

Business along the real Angels Branch was light for most of the line's existence. This was just as well, for the rugged terrain forced the builders to size the switchback tail tracks to hold only an engine, three cars, and a caboose. In fact, heavy trains (those hauling ore or timber) had only two cars plus a caboose.

The model track plan follows this prototype feature with switchback tail tracks only 24" long, just enough to fit a small engine and three cars. Longer trains could be run by doubling between Carson Hill and Melones, but you'd be well advised to bring along a lunch when trying this.

LOCOMOTIVES AND EQUIPMENT

The Sierra ran small engines and cars on the Angels Branch. Service was started with a Heisler, engine No. 9, which soon gave way to a couple of 60-ton Shays, Nos. 10 and 11. A 90-ton Shay, No. 12, joined this group of gear grinders before all yielded to rod engines.

A 42" drivered 2-6-2 Prairie from Baldwin, No. 30, arrived in 1922 and was followed the next year by another 2-6-2, No. 32. This was also Baldwin built, but had 46" drivers. The usual assignments on the Angels Branch saw No. 32 hauling freight and No. 30 passengers.

The Sierra interchanged freight cars

An Angel's Camp train crosses the Stanislaus River on the Melones trestle. Right of the train is a flume that carried water into the tank beside the track. Left is a 6' diameter pipe, made of redwood, that carried water on to the Melones Mine.

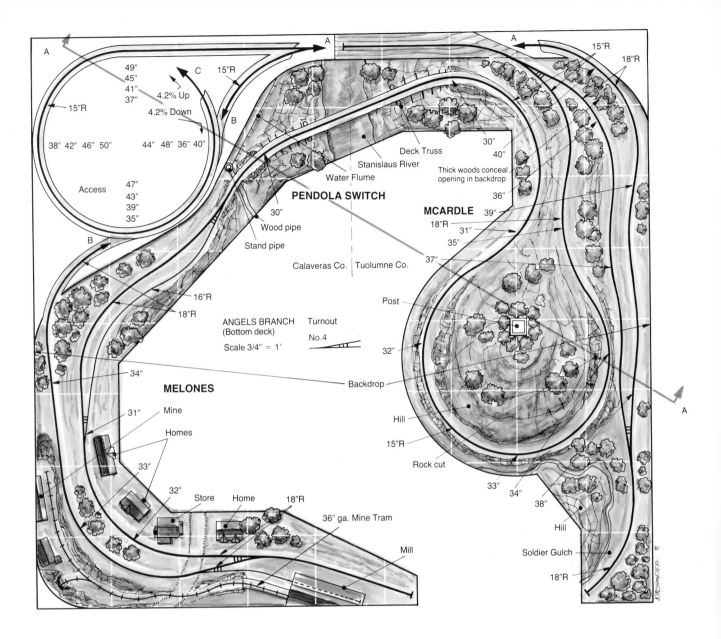

A
A
A
15"R
18"R

49"
45"
41"
37"
4.2% Up
C
15"R
4.2% Down
B

15"R
38" 42" 46" 50"   44" 48" 36" 40"
30"
40"
Access
47"
43"
39"
35"

Thick woods conceal
opening in backdrop

30"
Wood pipe
Deck Truss
Stanislaus River
Water Flume
36"

PENDOLA SWITCH

MCARDLE

18"R
31"
35"
37"

Stand pipe
Calaveras Co. | Tuolumne Co.

B
16"R
18"R

Post

32"

ANGELS BRANCH
(Bottom deck)
Scale 3/4" = 1'
Turnout
No.4

Backdrop

34"

MELONES

Hill

31"
Mine
15"R

Homes
Rock cut

33"
33" 34"
38"

32"
Store
Home
18"R

Hill

36" ga. Mine Tram

Soldier Gulch

Mill
18"R

A

KIRCHMEIER '91

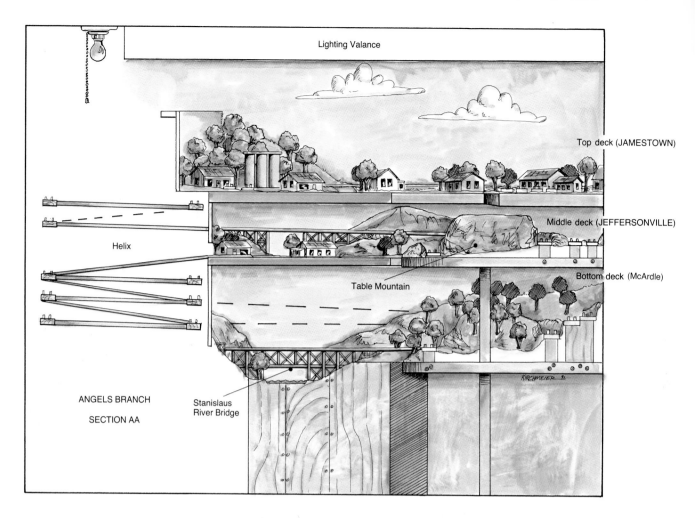

Lighting Valance

Top deck (JAMESTOWN)

Middle deck (JEFFERSONVILLE)

Helix

Bottom deck (McArdle)

Table Mountain

KIRCHMEIER 91

ANGELS BRANCH

SECTION AA

Stanislaus
River Bridge

with both the Southern Pacific and the Santa Fe in Oakdale, and these cars made their way to destinations on the branch. The tight curves and steep grades of the Angels Branch did lead to the acquisition of some unique shorty passenger cars, combine No. 5 and coach No. 6, for Jamestown-Angels Camp service.

Many models of Sierra Ry. engines and rolling stock have been produced. Besides imported brass models, Model Die Casting kits for short, old-time freight cars, passenger cars, and locomotives (including a Shay), are almost an ideal match for both the theme and the 15″-radius curves that Rick used for his Angels Branch plan.

VARIATIONS

The branch was abandoned in 1939, so only steam locomotives trod the rails between Jamestown and Angels Camp. No one says your Angels Branch couldn't outlast the prototype, though, and the Sierra did become noted for its use of Baldwin diesel switchers on the heavier mainline rail between Oakdale and Jamestown.

Rick has successfully operated Athearn switchers over radii down to 10″. With minor modifications to increase truck and coupler swing you could operate some small Baldwin diesels on the Angels Branch while still maintaining the prototype Sierra Ry. image.

The layout concept could be modified. By leaving out the middle deck you could make it smaller and simplify construction. Another variation would be to shorten the run and increase the minimum radius to 22″ by incorporating helixes at opposite corners of the room. As with the Union Pacific in Chapter 4, the key is using imagination and flexibility in mating helixes and decks to achieve the desired result.

THE SHENANGO VALLEY

An HO layout where scenery matters most

Not every modeler wants a layout with an extensive main line and a full complement of industrial spurs for switching operations. Some modelers may be more interested in emphasizing the scenery on their layout, wanting nothing more elaborate than a simple circular track design. But a circular track design poses a problem: How does one provide access to the inside of the circle?

There are several methods for attacking the access problem. A section of the railroad can be built on a hinged leaf that lifts up, drops down, or swings aside like a gate. Hinged leaves are an advantage because they can be switched rapidly from the closed position for op-

erating trains to the open position for ready access. Their disadvantages lie in the construction required to keep them in true alignment and in their reliance on flexible wiring or mating contacts to deliver electricity to the rails.

Lift-out sections can also be used to span an entryway. These sections are essentially hinged leaves without the hinges. Although they're easier to construct, installing and removing them takes longer.

Additionally, when appropriate to your railroad, a bascule or similar moving lift bridge can be used as a means of providing walk-in access to the inside of a layout. Moving bridges have the advantage of rapid and prototypical op-

eration, but the added construction work required is obvious.

Sometimes, however, none of these methods will work for your layout. Such was the case with the Shenango Valley (SV) RR. The requirements imposed on the design precluded using the above methods. No portion of the SV benchwork could be larger than 16″ x 72″. All sections had to fit together securely, yet be detachable in case the builder had to move. The available area of 7′ x 13′ had to accommodate an existing sump pump, a workbench, and the layout, as well as provide good access to all.

The primary goal was to simulate an upstate New York setting with empha-

Philip R. Hastings photo

Upstate New York is the setting for this 1950 branchline train just leaving Lake Clear Jct. on its way to Saranac Lake. The gentle hills and sparse structures are fairly typical of this area, a characteristic that should be reflected on the Shenango Valley RR.

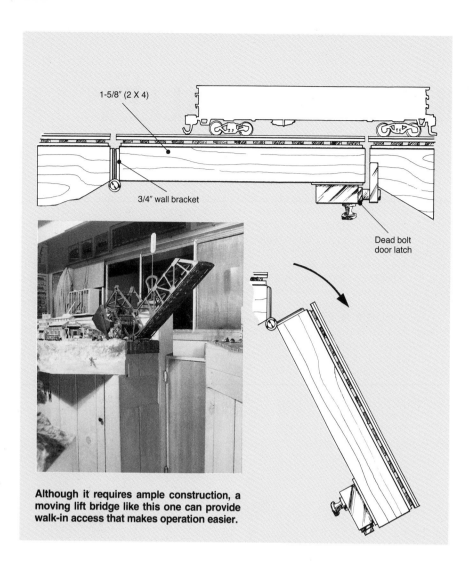

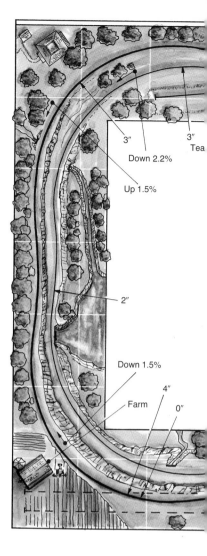

Although it requires ample construction, a moving lift bridge like this one can provide walk-in access that makes operation easier.

sis on scenery and structures. Railroad action was limited to a continuous-run shortline main with a possible interchange connection to one of the area main lines: NYO & W, DL & W, D & H, or NYC. To quote the builder's instructions, "Where in doubt, eliminate track."

A continuous-run on benchwork limited to 16″ wide dictated a circular track pattern. The emphasis on scenery provided the key for solving the access problem. In nature, the horizon is *always* at or above the eye level of the viewer. If the SV scenery was to give the illusion of the real world, the horizon line for the scenery had to be raised to the builder's eye level. Duplicating the relatively gentle slopes of New York on the narrow benchwork of the SV meant the track would be only a few inches below the horizon level. Working downward from this level establishes the lowest track at 56″ above the floor. This allows the central operating area to be reached by stooping under the layout even if walk-in access can't be provided. Scoot-under access is also possible if the workbench chair is equipped with casters.

The hidden storage tracks and interchange runaround were deliberately included despite the requirement to

minimize trackwork. Why? Because highly detailed scenery and structures will demand highly detailed rolling stock, and to preserve the fine details and weathering patina of this equipment, handling should be kept to a minimum. Storage tracks provide a place to keep such equipment without handling it on and off the layout. Moreover, if operation other than just running a train in a circle is ever desired, these tracks add the capability for switching, runaround, and interchange moves.

WALKAROUND TYPES

It may seem strange that a center operating pit design like that of the Shenango Valley has been included in a book about walkalong layouts, but in some cases the best model railroad will result when an entry or access path has to penetrate the track right of way. The walkaround nature of the remaining access aisles should be preserved, though.

Some clarifying terminology is in order at this point. "Walkaround" has been commonly used to describe model railroad layouts designed with continuous aisles allowing access for operation. It is a broad enough definition to allow pop-up access hatches for maintenance

in hard-to-reach locations. When no stoop-under or movable track section is required for entry, a walkaround design also becomes a "walk-in" layout. A walk-in walkaround design gives the best combination of access features.

From an operational viewpoint, a "walkalong" layout is very desirable. This features access aisles and track routes designed so an operator can walk along with the train being controlled. Aside from access considerations, this has the aesthetic advantage of simulating the prototype by having the engineer move through the scenery along with the train.

WALKAROUND PRINCIPLES

The small layouts described illustrate the basic principles of walkaround design. All of the larger walkaround layouts that follow are extensions of these principles:

• Provide continuous aisles along the layout edge.

• Keep trackwork within reach for both operation and maintenance.

• Adjust the height of the layout to the operator (or vice versa) to provide the best combination for accessible reach.

• Employ conventional layout design components non-conventionally to gain

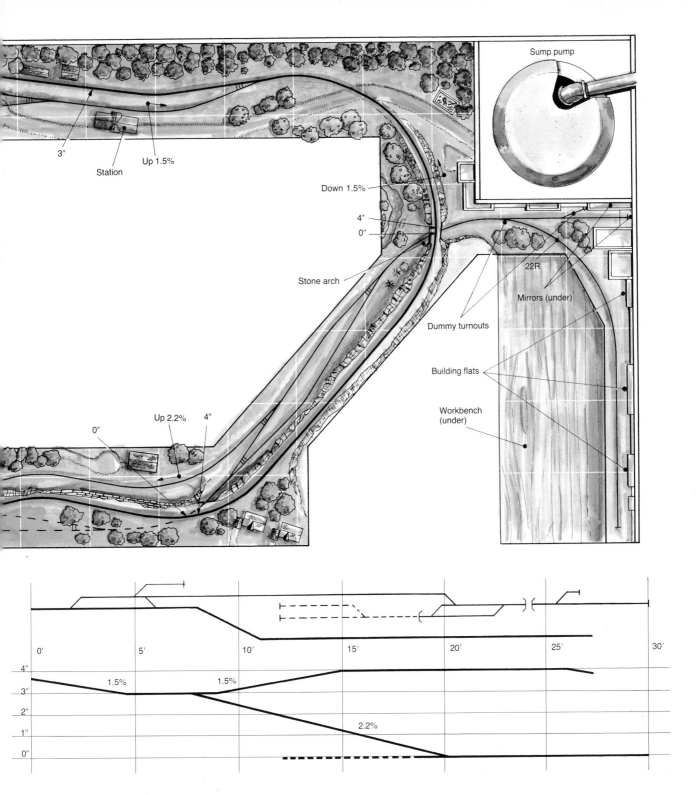

3″
Station
Up 1.5%
Sump pump
Down 1.5%
4″
0″
Stone arch
22R
Mirrors (under)
Dummy turnouts
Building flats
Workbench (under)
Up 2.2%   4″
0″

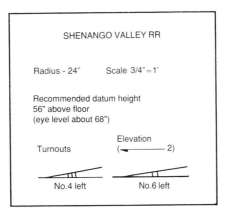

4″
3″
2″
1″
0″
0'   5'   1.5%   10'   1.5%   15'   2.2%   20'   25'   30'

maximum use of available space while preserving accessibility.

• Preserve walkaround access even if walk-in entry can't be provided.

These principles are not absolute. Some deviations are acceptable — even desirable — to achieve a specific operating or scenic goal. Too many deviations, however, can detract from the overall enjoyment of walkaround layout design by hindering operating and maintenance access. And at all costs, avoid separate operating spaces accessible only by crawling under the benchwork — these are the pits.

SHENANGO VALLEY RR

Radius - 24″   Scale 3/4″ = 1'

Recommended datum height
56″ above floor
(eye level about 68″)

Turnouts

Elevation
(⟵———— 2)

No.4 left   No.6 left

Layout at a glance

Name: SHENANGO VALLEY
Scale: HO
Space: 7' x 13' x 7'
Location: Basement corner
Operation: Display oval plus
Emphasis: Center access

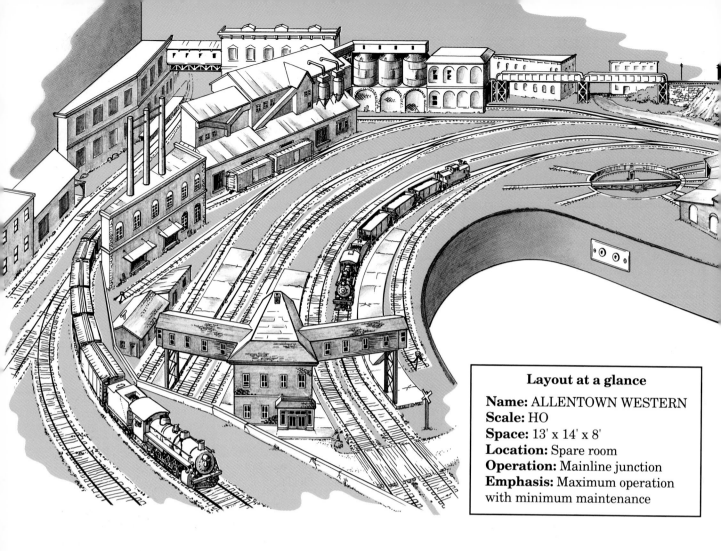

THE ALLENTOWN WESTERN

A medium-size HO layout with great operation potential

This track plan shows that it's possible to pack quite a bit of operating potential into a room-size layout space. By doing this with a modest amount of track, you ease maintenance chores to the point that continued operation is an enjoyable experience. The HO scale Allentown Western is based on ideas developed by John Allen after he had accumulated about ten years of experience on his famed Gorre & Daphetid Lines.

The best ways of ensuring that maintenance will be easy and infrequent are to design a layout with accessibility to all areas and to use high-quality, reliable materials. This second point is especially true for mechanisms like switch machines and electrical controls, which will be operated regularly. Whatever money is "saved" on such components before construction begins will likely be paid out many times over the long run by the time consumed making repairs

and replacing parts. The larger the layout or the smaller the maintenance crew, the more that expensive industrial-grade components prove to be a bargain.

THE TRACK PLAN

The basic route of this 13' x 14' layout is from a reversing loop at Johnsville down to another reversing loop at Allentown. Both of these towns have industrial spurs. There are also hidden tracks for a loads-in empties-out operation between the mine at Johnsville and the smelter at Allentown. These tracks form an alternative route for continuous running when desired. The main line between the two loops is a single track, with passing sidings and industrial spurs at Skyview and Whitby.

The heart-shaped operating area is determined by access considerations. The upper lobes place all the turnouts at Johnsville, Skyview, and Allentown

within reach. While the turnouts are within reach, both the Johnsville factory spur and the Skyview industry spur extend into the corners. Use of a stool or the emergency access hatch will be required if something goes wrong on the far reaches of these spurs.

The mountain ridge inside the turnback curve at the Whitby corner prevents any feasible reach from the center operating space, so the spur in this corner is a dummy track. A mirror set against the wall creates the illusion that this spur branches to a location beyond the wall. An emergency access hatch is built into the far side of the ridge for access to the main line. Another hatch is similarly worked into the scenery near the Johnsville mine, though the mine turnouts are located within reach of the operating aisle.

The engine facilities at Allentown are located up front to provide a scenic focal point as well as to place them

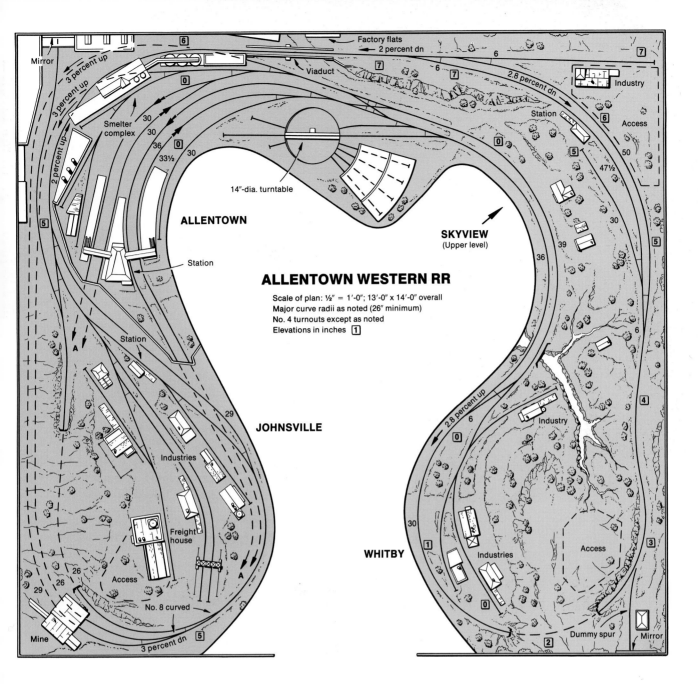

ALLENTOWN WESTERN RR

Scale of plan: ½″ = 1′-0″; 13′-0″ x 14′-0″ overall
Major curve radii as noted (26″ minimum)
No. 4 turnouts except as noted
Elevations in inches [1]

Mirror

3 percent up

2 percent up

Smelter complex

30
30
36
33½
30

14″-dia. turntable

ALLENTOWN

Station

Station

A

JOHNSVILLE

29

Industries

Freight house

Access

No. 8 curved

26
26
29

Mine

3 percent dn

5

A

Factory flats
2 percent dn

6

Viaduct

7
6
7

2.8 percent dn

Station

6

Industry

Access

50

47½

30

SKYVIEW
(Upper level)

39

36

5

6

4

2.8 percent up

6

Industry

0

30

1

WHITBY

Industries

0

Access

3

Dummy spur

Mirror

2

within easy reach. Up-front activities, such as the engine terminal and passenger station, draw eyes from the flats and partial buildings that make up the smelter complex. As a result, the overall scenic illusion is more believable.

Allentown itself represents a busy junction of two lines. Simulating the heavy operation that would occur at such a junction requires the use of staging tracks. Staging tracks, hidden or visible, are an old idea in layout design but are most often seen in the form of parallel yard tracks. The space and

simplicity concepts behind the layout's design dictated the use of the Allentown reversing loop for linear staging of trains.

OPERATION

Each loop track is about 28′ long be-

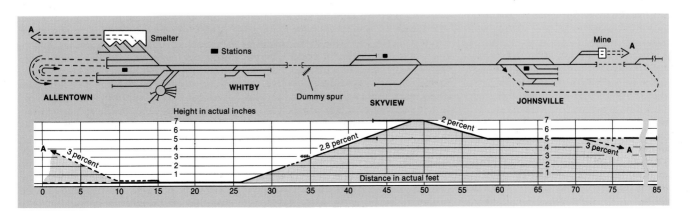

A
Smelter
Stations
Mine
A

ALLENTOWN
WHITBY
Dummy spur
SKYVIEW
JOHNSVILLE

Height in actual inches

7
6
5
4
3
2
1

2 percent

2.8 percent

A
3 percent

3 percent
A

Distance in actual feet

0   5   10   15   20   25   30   35   40   45   50   55   60   65   70   75   80   85

This mining operation served by the Kennecott rail line in Nevada is a good model for the AW.

tween clearance points at the turnouts. By electrically gapping the tracks into four 7′ sections and limiting trains to about 6′ in length (nine 40-foot cars, along with a locomotive and a caboose), it's possible to hold three trains on each loop track and still have room for an arriving one. Two trains can be concealed on the hidden portion of each track.

Operation of the hidden track can best be accomplished by observing the one-way traffic directions indicated by the arrows on the plan. The simplest linear staging operation consists of running the first train into the hidden track until the engine is sighted at the exit tunnel portal. The second train follows on the same track until its caboose disappears into the entrance tunnel portal. This operation could be automated by installing detection and stop/advance circuitry.

Arriving trains are alternated between the clockwise and counterclockwise loop tracks. An arrival triggers the departure of a train from the far end of the arriving track. At a suitable time after the departure, all the trains on that track are moved up to make room for the next arrival. In between these staging movements you can do local industrial switching.

Meanwhile, out on the main line, the departing train switches the on-line industries or makes station stops as appropriate. Throw in some meets with other trains, including unit ore trains running between the mine and the smelter, and there should be enough action to suit the most die-hard operating enthusiast.

It's another scorcher in California's Owens Valley, and it's another run for the Slim Princess, nearing the end of its service in this 1959 photo.

CARSON & COLORADO

A narrow gauge railroad that climbs like its prototype

Narrow gauge enthusiasts have long lavished their attention on the romantic railroads of the Colorado, but other narrow gauge common carriers operated east of Denver and west of Salt Lake. The one that operated the longest was, like the Denver & Rio Grande narrow gauge, part of a major railroad system. The Southern Pacific narrow gauge, revered as The Slim Princess, ran the 70 miles between Keeler and Laws in California's Owens Valley until its rails were pulled up from the sandy desert floor in 1960.

The Slim Princess was the dream of three Comstock Lode tycoons associated with the Virginia & Truckee: Darius Ogden Mills, William Sharon, and Henry Yerington. Spurred on by Sharon, the line owed its construction more to the afterglow of the Comstock bonanza than to any solid traffic sources then in existence. Shortly after completion of the line to its southern terminus of Keeler, the three men made a two-day trip to assess the economic prospects for their railroad. Mills' remark to his partners on that occasion has become a permanent part of railroad lore: "Gentlemen, either we have built this line 300 miles too long or 300 years too soon."

The 1980s, however, provide considerably brighter economic prospects for a model of the Carson & Colorado. Here's the story of how one railroad got started.

The accumulated artifacts of several years of modeling in HO were successfully swapped for On3 brass locomotives of C & C and Southern Pacific prototypes: a 4-4-0, a 2-8-0, and two 4-6-0s. Right-of-way was available in a basement room, and a 2'-wide shelf area was also available in the other half of the basement.

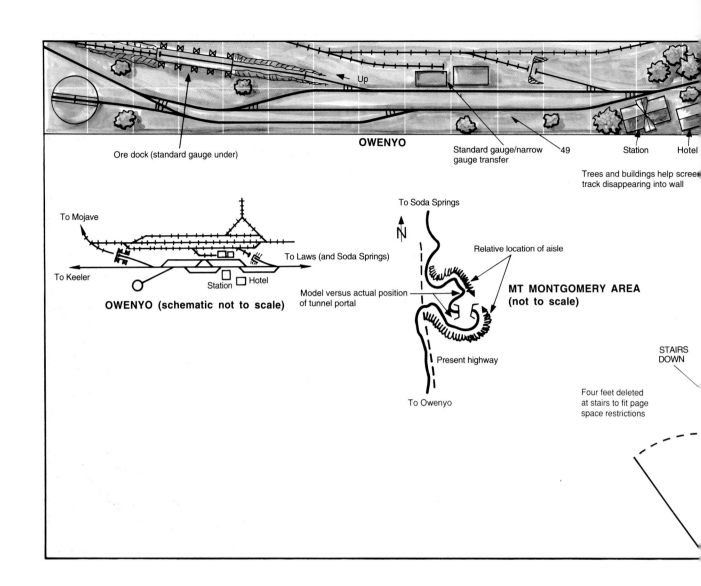

OWENYO

Ore dock (standard gauge under)

Standard gauge/narrow gauge transfer

49

Station   Hotel

Trees and buildings help screen track disappearing into wall

To Mojave

To Keeler

To Laws (and Soda Springs)

Station   Hotel

OWENYO (schematic not to scale)

To Soda Springs

N

Relative location of aisle

Model versus actual position of tunnel portal

MT MONTGOMERY AREA (not to scale)

Present highway

To Owenyo

STAIRS DOWN

Four feet deleted at stairs to fit page space restrictions

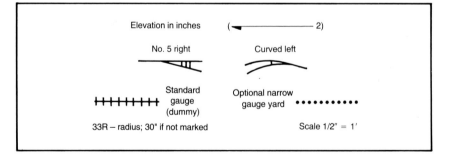

Layout at a glance
Name: CARSON & COLORADO
Scale: On3
Location: Divided basement
Operation: Desert narrow gauge
Emphasis: Platform access to high layout

Elevation in inches   (⟵————— 2)

No. 5 right   Curved left

Standard gauge (dummy)

Optional narrow gauge yard   •••••••••

33R – radius; 30" if not marked

Scale 1/2″ = 1′

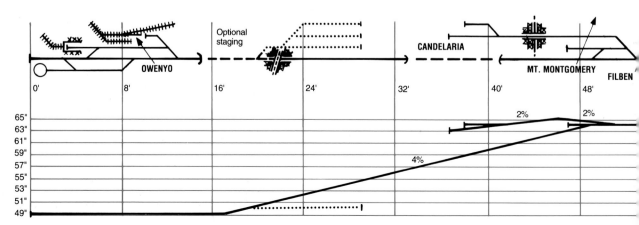

Optional staging

CANDELARIA

OWENYO

MT. MONTGOMERY

FILBEN

0'   8'   16'   24'   32'   40'   48'

2%   2%

65"
63"
61"
59"
57"   4%
55"
53"
51"
49"

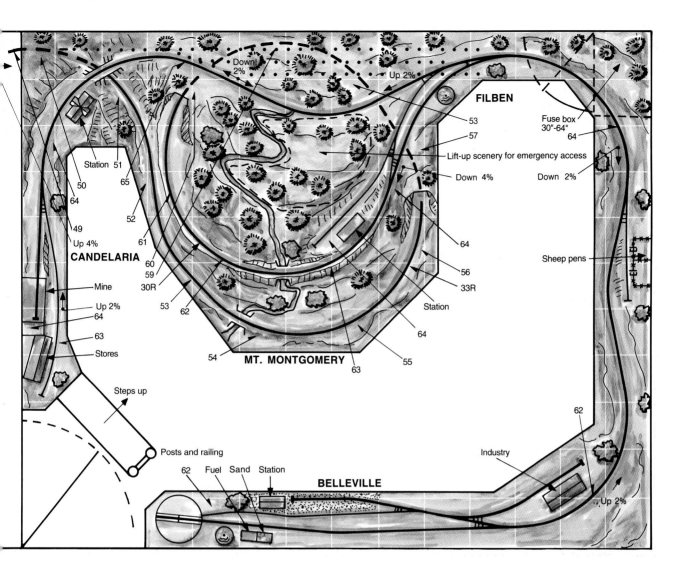

Station 51
50
65
64
52
49
Up 4%
61
CANDELARIA
60
59
Mine
30R
Up 2%
53
64
62
63
Stores

Down 2%
Up 2%

FILBEN
53
57
Fuse box
30"-64"
64
Lift-up scenery for emergency access
Down 4%
Down 2%
64
56
33R
Station
64

Sheep pens

54
MT. MONTGOMERY
63
55

62

Steps up

Posts and railing
62   Fuel   Sand   Station
Industry
BELLEVILLE
Up 2%

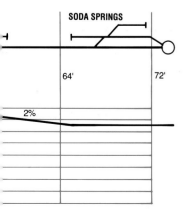

SODA SPRINGS

64'   72'

2%

The challenges to a suitable layout design were fairly clear-cut. A physical obstacle was posed by an electrical supply cabinet extending between 30″ and 64″ above the basement floor. Access to this cabinet in the far corner had to be maintained. The builder wanted the layout suitable for the eras of the brass locomotives: 1900–1910 for the Carson & Colorado and 1930–1940 for the Southern Pacific narrow gauge. A standard gauge interchange also had to be represented.

The layout design seemed to just fall in place from the combination of prototype features and model desires. The prototype reached a summit of 7,141′ on Mt. Montgomery. The summit of the model was determined by the height of the electrical supply cabinet. Mt. Montgomery became a natural selection for the main feature of the layout.

A one-turn helix provided the model with both a semi-prototypic orientation (see track plan) and a means of bringing the track down to a lower height. A 36″ minimum radius was considered, but would have eliminated both the branch and access aisle at Candelaria. The 30″ radius was chosen only after it was determined the two 4-6-0s could be made to run satisfactorily on such curves. This permitted the retention of the narrow aisle at Candelaria as well as holding the other aisle width at 3′.

The space under Mt. Montgomery was large enough to include an optional hidden yard. This could be used either for staging trains during operation or for on-track storage of unused equipment.

After Mt. Montgomery was located, the narrow shelves for Candelaria and Soda Springs were connected. The track at all these locations contains prototypic features without attempting to model specifics. Candelaria was a mining town, and a turntable was once at Belleville. Filben was the departure point for the branch to Candelaria, but it was further from Mt. Montgomery than represented on the model. The passing siding here is more of a run-around track to allow switching of the branch and station spur by trains headed in either direction.

Pushing the track elevation up to 64″ over the electrical cabinet meant that the height relationship between the layout and the builder had to be adjusted. This called for a raised operating aisle, with the 12″ platform height chosen so the layout fell somewhere between the elbow and underarm. The illustration on page 30 shows the sight

Ten-wheeler No. 22 was the most powerful engine to run on the Slim Princess. The 4-6-0 was so heavy it broke rails during the bitter cold winters experienced in the high desert.

line considerations that also applied.

The platform required two steps, at 6″ each, which neatly fit the ergonomically recommended range of 6″-7.5″. A post and rail protect one side of the stairway while preserving access to the turntable at Soda Springs. The layout corner at Candelaria was flared out into the aisle to provide warning for the other side of the stairway.

The 4 percent helix grade also seemed to fall in place. It provided adequate clearance between the stacked levels of track while duplicating the prototype grade. The steepness furnishes a reason for short trains and doubleheading on the model just as it did on the prototype. The overall elevation change in the helix brought the track height down to 49″ for the continuation onto the shelf in the other half of the basement.

That shelf was a suitable location for simulating the SP standard gauge interchange at Owenyo. Even with the standard gauge represented by dummy trackage, it was still possible to give a good sense of the prototype scene (see schematic). There was enough space, too, for inclusion of a model or the ore transfer dock scaled from on-site measurements of the prototype ruins.

Who knows? If Darius Mills had been a model railroader, he may have never uttered those famous words.

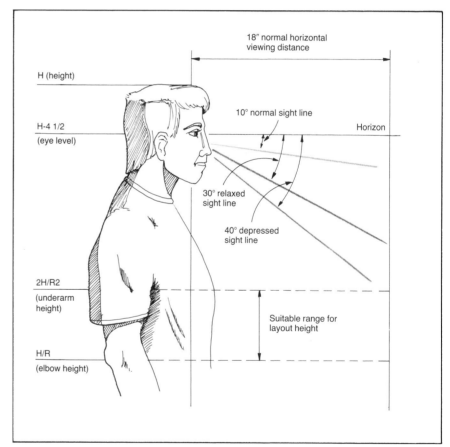

Santa Fe Ry.

Action and smoke billowing from hardworking engines and helpers — that's what Raton Pass was all about in the glory days of steam. Here two trains meet on the double-tracked pass.

RATON PASS

An HO layout featuring double-track Santa Fe action

Model Railroaders have always been partial to the Atchison, Topeka & Santa Fe Ry, known for its colorful western image. Just the sheer size of the system — it stretches from Lake Michigan to the Gulf of Mexico and the Pacific Ocean — is attractive to many, and you can add to that the enormous diversity of its operations. But that same immensity and diversity makes it difficult to choose a specific locale and type of operation — the possibilities seem endless.

Take this railroad. I designed it for a man who wanted a double-track main line to permit one-man operation of several trains simultaneously. How-

ever, even that didn't limit the choices much — you can find a lot of double track on the Santa Fe.

HEAD FOR THE HILLS

How then to choose the specific location? For starters, mountainous terrain is particularly desirable for a model railroad. Besides being inherently interesting, hills justify and also help hide the unrealistic turnback curves so often needed to fit a model railroad into the available space.

Rugged topography also helps justify the grades we use to gain multiple levels of track, and it lends credence to the tunnels we need to lead trains "offstage"

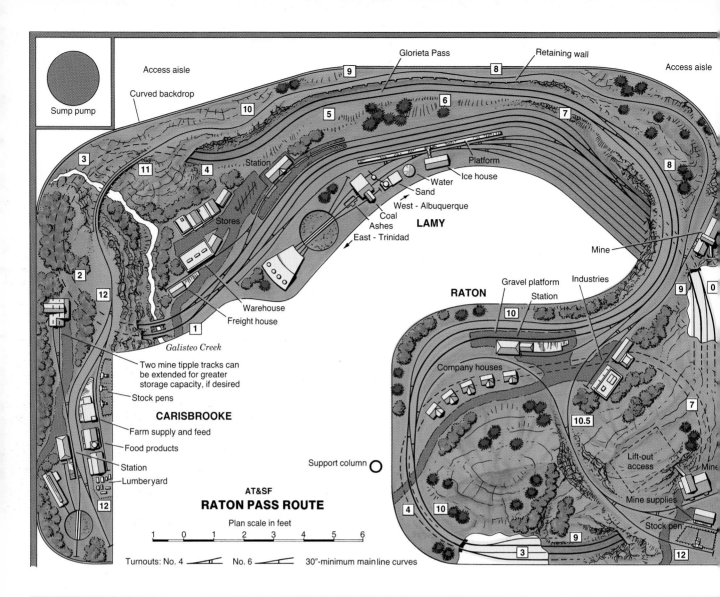

Access aisle

Curved backdrop

Sump pump

Glorieta Pass

Retaining wall

Access aisle

Station

LAMY

Platform

Ice house

Water

Sand

West - Albuquerque

Coal

Ashes

East - Trinidad

Stores

Warehouse

Freight house

Galisteo Creek

Two mine tipple tracks can
be extended for greater
storage capacity, if desired

Stock pens

CARISBROOKE

Farm supply and feed

Food products

Station

Lumberyard

Support column

AT&SF
RATON PASS ROUTE

Plan scale in feet

1   0   1   2   3   4   5   6

Turnouts: No. 4 ⌐ No. 6 ⌐   30″-minimum mainline curves

Mine

RATON

Gravel platform

Industries

Station

Company houses

10.5

Lift-out
access

Mine

Mine supplies

Stock pen

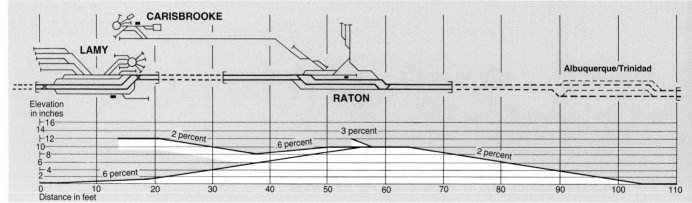

CARISBROOKE

LAMY

RATON

Albuquerque/Trinidad

Elevation
in inches

2 percent

.6 percent

3 percent

2 percent

.6 percent

Distance in feet

Layout at a glance

Name: RATON PASS
Scale: HO
Space: 17' x 22' x 8'
Location: Basement rec room
Operation: Mainline double track and branch
Emphasis: Operating alternatives

during operating sessions. Often we must run tracks that are theoretically miles apart within a few feet — or even a few inches — of each other. Separating such tracks vertically helps provide visual justification for their proximity.

Mountain scenery also solves many backdrop problems. In fact, if the mountain scenery extends above the horizon, the backdrop need only be painted a sky color. Below eye level, some talented artistry may be required, or you can use

one of the printed backdrops that are available commercially.

THE PERFECT PASS

With the Santa Fe, double track, and hilly terrain in mind, what could be a more suitable setting for a model railroad than famed Raton Pass? (Raton is pronounced "rah-TONE," with the accent on the second syllable. It's Spanish for "large mouse"!) Located on the border between New Mexico and Colorado, the route was laid out in 1878 and has

been used ever since, although traffic has been light since the 1940s. (Alternate routes have easier grades).

The prototype area certainly has the rugged terrain suited to model railroads, and railroad action was plentiful in earlier days, with lots of double- and triple-heading to get the trains over the hill. Freight and passenger trains were mixed in with helper movements. Branch lines served the mining districts in the area, and that's another advantage for layout design purposes. Junctions work well in almost any size space because they present multiple opportunities. You can emphasize the main line, the branch, or both for operating and scenic purposes.

In this case the focus of the model main line was to be on continuous running, but including a branch permitted the addition of switching operations.

DESIGN CONSIDERATIONS

The Raton Pass layout plan had to combine double track with single-person, walkaround operation. The desired minimum radii were 30″ on the main line and 24″ on the branch. The space available for it was a 17′ x 22′ area at one end of a basement recreation room.

In addition, part of this area had to accommodate one end of a Ping Pong table, though it could double as a layout entry.

Double track on a model railroad can pose visual problems because it tends to dominate everything else. We need to use some tricks to counteract this "too much track" feeling.

One good ploy is to give double track (and single track) a flowing look by using a lot of curvature. The eye can take in a long, straight stretch at a glance, but must linger longer over a series of curves. Be sure, however, that your alternating curves don't lead directly into each other. The reverse or "S" curves so formed can cause derailments. A stretch of straight track at least as long as the longest engine or car should be located between such reverse curves.

THE BASIC CONCEPT

The track plan is straightforward. Starting at the bottom of the hill there's a station with passing tracks, engine facilities, and a small yard. Next comes the climb up the hill. Then there's a summit station with a mainline passing track and a helper wye leading into a branch line. Just past the summit, a tunnel leads into hidden staging tracks that connect back to the base station.

The wye and branch were laid out with a twofold objective: to create a single-track switching counterpoint to the double-track mainline running, and to make it easy to add a possible future connection around the remainder of the recreation room.

Fitting the layout into the space available didn't look like it would be too tough, but there were some complicating factors. In one rear corner was a sump pump. Given Murphy's Law ("If something can go wrong, it will"), that sump pump was destined to break down just as soon as a big, beautiful portion of layout blocking access to it was completed.

Working space for a plumber was therefore an essential part of the design. With the sump pump access space located in one corner, it followed that a narrow access aisle could be extended full-length along the back of the layout. This aisle would provide easy access to the trackwork and scenery from the rear, meaning the benchwork in front of it could be relatively wide. This rear aisle would not have to be particularly spacious, though, as it would see only occasional use for plumbing, maintenance, or access to trains in trouble.

If the layout were to be built much lower than eye level, a profile board

high as possible above the floor to provide the best combination of access and scenic realism. The higher the benchwork, the easier it will be to get underneath — remember, the plumber may have to get to that sump pump! A high layout also makes the branch terminal at Carisbrooke less likely to be damaged by players lunging for a Ping Pong ball.

The scenery should reflect the Colorado-New Mexico border area. It's not what you'd call heavily forested, but it's not a desert either. I've shown a considerable number of trees and other vegetation around Carisbrooke for variety. The dry bed of Galisteo Creek (appropriately originating near the sump pump) helps separate Carisbrooke from the lower level at Lamy. The high trestle tucked in the corner further accentuates the visual separation.

OPERATION

One-person operation of a relatively large railroad requires design trade-offs. I located the trackage at Raton directly across from Lamy to make operation of both more convenient for one person. If the railroad was to be for multiple operation, it would be better to move Raton closer to the tunnel entrance, resulting in less operator congestion and a longer visible run between stations.

The one-person operating scheme is simple. A train can be set up for continuous running on one of the double-track lines, while the operator uses the other main for adding or removing helpers, timetable operation, or switching. Or the operator can set trains running continuously on both mains and operate the branch. A little variety can be introduced by using the hidden staging tracks to alternate trains. More variety can be added by using the stub end yard at Lamy for breaking down and making up trains.

CONTROLS

Tethered throttles on 15′ cords would work well on this layout. For easy access to any point on the layout such throttles could be connected to the layout near the house support pillar at Raton. Electrical controls for block selection could also be located near the pillar, with additional local controls at Raton, Lamy, and Carisbrooke.

Since walkaround design puts the operator where the train is, most of the turnouts can be hand-thrown, reducing the need for large control panels. This will also reduce the amount of wiring, number of electrical components, and cost. Only the turnouts on the hidden storage tracks and the wye tail require some form of remote control.

There you have it, a basement-size Santa Fe with as much action as any one person — or any several — can handle. Can't you just see those double-headed steamers slugging it out with the hill?

Phillip R. Hastings

A helper shoves as a freight train works through the twin tunnels at the top of the pass. The puff of smoke on the hillside ahead is coming from the train's lead engine through a ventilator shaft.

painted with a continuation of the scenery should be erected along the rear of the benchwork. The upper edge of the profile board should have a rolling contour to simulate hilltops and extend up to or above eye level.

The turnouts were located within a 30″ reach zone from the edge of the regular operating space, with the exception of the tail of the Raton wye. Turnouts are especially subject to Murphy's Law. A layout designed for operation must have them, but they are moving mechanisms that will eventually require maintenance to keep them operating properly. Those that are hardest to reach will invariably be the ones that give the most trouble. Providing easy access to turnouts is essential, so the wye-tail turnout at Raton needs to have a lift-out hatch located in the nearby hills.

Keeping in mind good ergonomics (the relationship between man and machine), the benchwork should be built as

A Spokane, Portland & Seattle 4-6-6-4 beats uphill at Marshall, Washington, in 1964. The quiet beauty of the Pacific Northwest is the setting for the Anon & Muss.

Dr Philip Hastings photo

ANON & MUSS

An HO single-track railroad that permits easy operation of several trains simultaneously

A relaxing evening with a model railroad can be a powerful antidote to a tough day at work. But it's hard to relax with your model railroad if its operation isn't hassle free. And although no-hassle operation is certainly attainable, it shouldn't, as it often does, diminish the number of trains you can run on your layout or severely limit other operating options. This notion is reflected in the premise behind the Anon & Muss's track plan: You *can* have easy operation even with several

trains running simultaneously on single track. Let's look at how the seemingly contradictory goal of the Anon & Muss was achieved.

Just so things wouldn't seem too easy, the following restrictions were placed on building the railroad: minimum radii of 32″ and 26″ for the main line and branch line, respectively; all turnouts No. 6 or larger; grades averaging 1.5 percent with a 2 percent maximum on the main line, and 2 per-

cent average with a 2.5 percent maximum on the branch; and sidings and yard tracks sized to handle 12–18-car trains. All this had to be blended together with scenery suggestive of the Pacific Northwest.

Doodling around with 32″-radius circles on a scale drawing quickly showed what could be done in the layout space. Walkaround access could be maintained only by some combination of track loops in the four corners and center of the room. Further sketching illustrated that the best access pattern was a

"Y"-shaped aisle leading in from the open end of the layout room. Once the aisle was established, an "E"-shaped pattern was left for the layout.

Several attempts were made at fitting a railroad into the "E" pattern, but none met the no-hassle, single-track goal. Suddenly, inspiration struck! Make the layout two separate lines. Interconnections between lines would allow the layout to be run as one railroad. Each route could be constructed independently if the lines were judiciously located in relation to each other.

CONSTRUCTION I

There is much to recommend designing a layout so that construction can occur in specific phases. Although it's still best to start preparing the railroad room before beginning the benchwork, phased construction may allow you to delay finishing all the room work. Likewise, with phased construction you can lay track before all the benchwork is completed, meaning the thrill of getting those trains running can come earlier.

Preparation of a layout room should start from the top down — ceiling, wiring and lights, backdrop — but construction of the layout itself is best started at the lowest level. On the A&M, this was the folded figure-8 portion (see sketch on page 38) incorporating the main yard at Anon.

The number of tracks in the yard was determined by the width of the benchwork left after establishing a 3' aisle width. The track pattern was determined by the desire to include two double-crossovers acquired for a previous layout plan. Two prized passenger trains of differing eras required suitable display, so the passenger station and associated storage tracks were located at the open entry end of the layout. An engine-house, turntable, and engine service buildings completed the railroad facilities at Anon.

The passing siding at Marcan Junction is not required for no-hassle operation. Later on, however, more operating flexibility will probably be desired; adding the passing siding at the beginning will make it easier to gain this. Without it, only one train at a time can run on the phase one trackage. The siding provides a meeting place for two trains about halfway between opposite ends of Anon.

The tracks leading under the siding to the Cognito Power Plant are an essential part of phase one construction. These tracks provide an independent yard switching lead, allowing yard movements to be made while a train is running on the main line. They also can be used as a location for trying some industry switching, or as overflow yard storage tracks.

<table>
<tr><td colspan="2">Layout at a glance</td></tr>
<tr><td>Name: ANON & MUSS</td></tr>
<tr><td>Scale: HO</td></tr>
<tr><td>Space: 16' x 24' x 7'6"</td></tr>
<tr><td>Location: Basement</td></tr>
<tr><td>Operation: Continuous-run single track with multiple trains</td></tr>
<tr><td>Emphasis: Phased construction</td></tr>
</table>

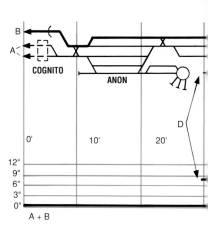

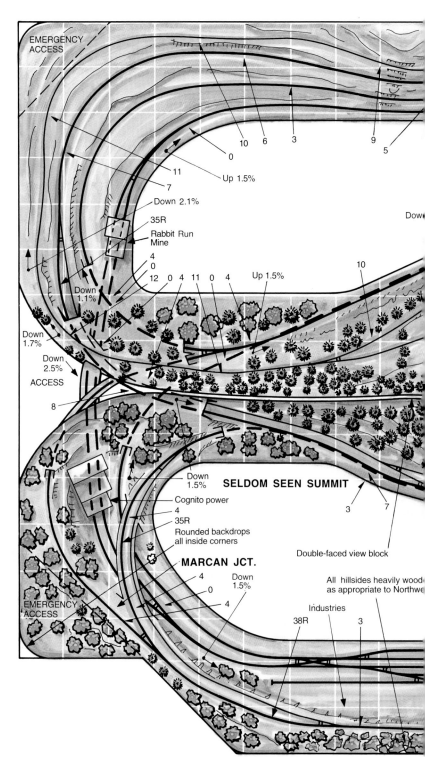

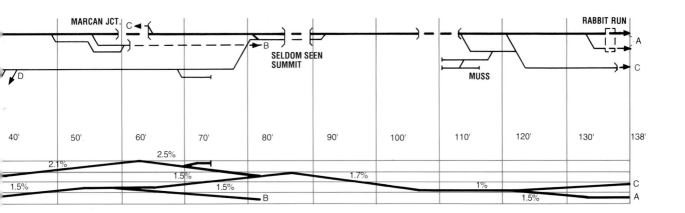

MARCAN JCT. C

SELDOM SEEN SUMMIT

B

D

RABBIT RUN
A
MUSS
C

40'	50'	60'	70'	80'	90'	100'	110'	120'	130'	138'

2.5%

2.1%

1.5%

1.7%

1.5%

1.5%

1.5%

1%

1.5%

C
A
B

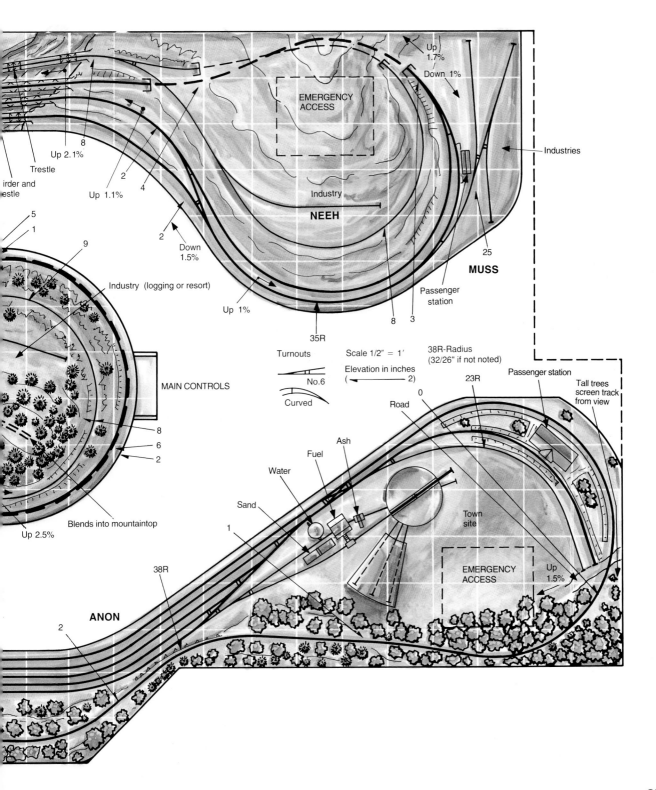

Up 1.7%

Down 1%

Industries

EMERGENCY ACCESS

Up 2.1%

Trestle

irder and
estle

Up 1.1%

8

2

4

2

Industry

NEEH

25

MUSS

Down 1.5%

Up 1%

8

3

Passenger station

35R

5

1

9

Industry (logging or resort)

MAIN CONTROLS

8

6

2

Blends into mountaintop

Up 2.5%

Turnouts

No.6

Curved

Scale 1/2″ = 1′

Elevation in inches
(——— 2)

38R-Radius
(32/26″ if not noted)

23R

Passenger station

Tall trees
screen track
from view

Road

Ash

0

Fuel

Water

Town
site

Sand

EMERGENCY ACCESS

Up 1.5%

1

38R

ANON

2

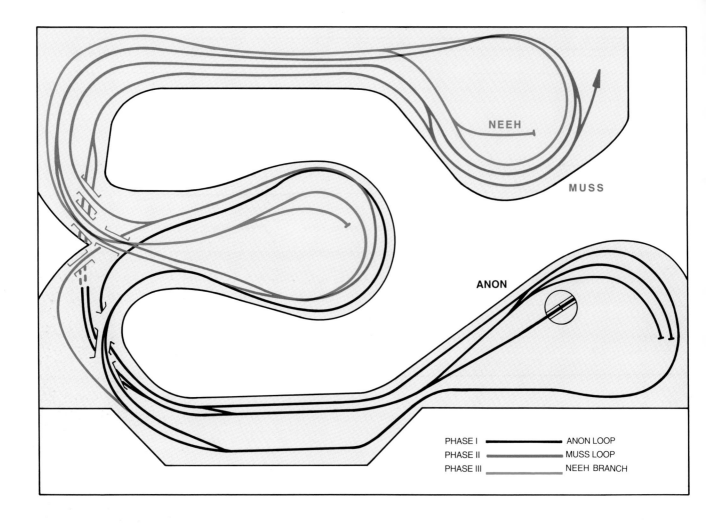

PHASE I	ANON LOOP
PHASE II	MUSS LOOP
PHASE III	NEEH BRANCH

CONSTRUCTION II

Once the Anon loop is operating, attention can shift to construction of the Muss loop. Remaining room preparation should be completed before benchwork is started on this portion of the layout. The bottom level tracks between Cognito and Rabbit Run mine should be extended first. Next up is the connection from Marcan Jct., and then the tracks on the center peninsula immediately above the Anon loop. The remainder of the Muss loop can be built in whatever order is convenient.

The Muss loop can be run completely independent of the Anon loop. Passing sidings at Muss and Seldom Seem Summit allow for two-train operation when desired. The latter siding is also the eventual connection point for the branch line. A few industrial spurs at Muss provide a chance for switching maneuvers when the mood strikes.

The Marcan Jct. and power plant/mine connections provide a means of linking the two loops. They can be used as part of a long continuous run (see schematic) or as part of a loaded/empty car exchange scheme. In the latter, loaded hoppers issue from Rabbit Run. From there they must be hauled up the grade through the passing track at Muss to the crest at Seldom Seem Summit tunnel. Dragging loaded hoppers up this hill provides justification

for the use of powerful locomotives on short trains. Once over the summit, the run is downhill, diverging from the Muss loop at the Marcan Jct. connection. Proceeding through the Anon yard, the hoppers are run *in cognito* until it is time to pull them out again. Empties travel the same route in the opposite direction.

CONSTRUCTION III

The final phase of construction is the branch line. It is connected to the Muss loop at Seldom Seem Summit and runs to a reversing loop at Neeh. The branch requires operator attention because of the out-and-back nature of the reverse-loop operation.

Spurs were included at Neeh and near Seldom Seem Summit on the branch to permit an independent back-and-forth operation between related industries. In such an operation, the reverse loop would only be used for positioning the engine on the proper end of the train for switching the spurs. A logging camp and a sawmill would make a good pair of related industries that fit well with the Northwest scenic theme. Space is available for adding more spurs at both locations should the desire for switching operation increase as experience with the railroad grows.

CONTROLS

The controls recommended for the

Anon & Muss were similar to those on the Raton Pass. The best location for a mainline control panel with tethered throttles is at the top of the center peninsula. This panel should contain the turnout and block controls as well. An auxiliary control panel for turntable operation is best located near the engine facility.

Three throttles were envisioned: one each for the Anon loop, the Muss loop, and the branch line. Each loop was divided into mainline electrical blocks between passing sidings or yard tracks. The passing sidings and yard tracks were also gapped as separate electrical blocks. This was probably a bit more than needed for no-hassle operation, but model railroads have a way of growing. Electrical gapping and connections for multi-train operation are better set up at the beginning. The blocks thus created can be wired together until the time arrives when individual block control switches become operationally desirable.

CUTTING CORNERS

The Anon & Muss does contain deviations from my espoused walkaround design principles. Although the "Y"-shaped aisle provides walk-in walk-around access, both aisles narrow as they diverge and wrap around the center peninsula. The Anon aisle is wider

Logging operations once permeated the backwoods along the branch lines of the Northwest.

because more operator traffic will occur in the vicinity of the yard.

Narrowness is a relative term when used to describe aisle width. Good ergonomic design holds that aisle size should be related to usage. The table lists some of these widths adapted for model railroad design. The goal for the A&M, as for most of the layouts in this book, was a minimum operating aisle width of 36″. This is not a rigid criterion; deviations are certainly acceptable where the overall result is a better model railroad.

Layout corners and peninsula lobes are two areas where the far reaches of scenery and track can exceed easy reach from an operating aisle. A provision for occasional access must be included in these locations. The A&M needs such access in both closed room corners and in both town lobes.

Access hatches come in all sizes and shapes dependent on layout conditions, so ergonomic design principles only suggest dimensions to be used. A rectangular hatch should be a minimum of 15″ x 20″ for the average man, while a round or square hatch should have a 20″ minimum diameter or side. The smallest ergonomically recommended hatch is a 10″ x 18″ oval, but using a hatch this small may limit the work that can be accomplished.

Dimensions should be increased if frequent use is anticipated, or for larger-than-average users. Also use bigger hatches where access from underneath

is restricted, as on vertically stacked layouts, or where a step has to be mounted to raise the user to a suitable working height above the surrounding layout features. Deviations in hatch sizes should

be employed if a better layout will result. As is the case with other dimensions suggested by ergonomic design, keep track of deviations so their number doesn't become unnecessarily large.

SUGGESTED AISLE WIDTHS

Width	Usage
16″	Sideways passage between two layout edges
20″	Sideways passage between wall and high backdrop
22″	Walking passage between two layout edges
24″	Sideways passage between wall (or high backdrop) and layout edge
26″	Walking passage between wall and high backdrop
28″	Two persons passing sideways between wall and high backdrop
30″	One-way passage on stairs or ramp between wall and high backdrop
32″	Rising from stool or armless chair between chair back and control panel or layout edge
36″	Bending space for under-layout access. Walking passage between wall and layout edge. Minimum aisle for wheelchair or two-crutch support
38″	Passage for two people between layout edges, one standing sideways
52″	Passage for two people walking between layout edges
96″	Public passageways

Note: Dimensions may be narrowed where it results in a better model railroad. Hold these deviations to a minimum, and limit traffic bottlenecks. Bottlenecks are likely to occur at entrances and exits, at the ends of stub aisles, and at busy locations like those adjacent to yards or other operation focal points.

The Chicago & North Western railroad served as the inspiration for the Omaha & North Western. Here a C&NW 4-6-0 local freight heads westbound just outside of O'Neil, Nebraska, on Labor Day, 1950.

THE OMAHA & NORTH WESTERN

A plan for all reasons

The Omaha & North Western Line evolved from the same struggle that confronts most potential model railroad builders: the attempt to resolve the differences between what is desired in a layout and what is feasible to actually build. Since the O&NW has many specific features included in its design that aren't apparent from looking at the track plan, it's worth looking into the design process to see how they were arrived at.

It's my belief that the logical first step in developing any plan is to list the desired features on paper. For the O&NW, these were:

● A midwestern locale with some flavor of the Chicago & North Western Ry.

● A single-track railroad with at least one branch line.

● Sufficient spurs and sidings to provide interesting operation.

● Radii large enough to handle all but the largest locomotives from the standpoint of both operation and appearance.

● Excellent access for operation.

● Construction, maintenance, and operation of the railroad to be within the capability of one man. . .

● . . . while, at the same time, suitably challenging to engage the diverse abilities of a small (10- to 15-member) club group.

● A total model railroad that would encourage and permit the participation of the builder's wife and two young sons.

Another list was prepared which noted the limitations:

● The physical dimensions of the layout room.

● Free passageway must be maintained between the two doors in the room when the layout is not in use.

● The cost of components had to be minimized in order to remain within a limited budget.

From these two lists it should be readily apparent that there were a great many compromises which had to be reasoned out. This was particularly

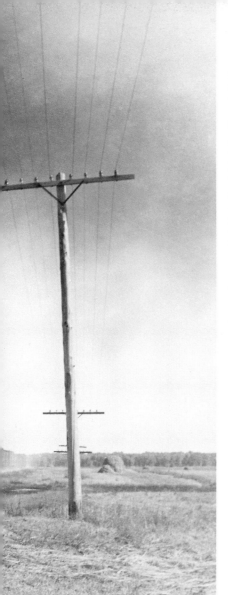

ACCESS

Before this matching process could come into play, however, some rough sketches quickly revealed that use of the minimum radii specified in Table 11-1 would present major problems. The desired walk-in aisles and other access requirements could not be met using a 36″ radius on the main line. More attempts at sketching alternatives were made using progressively smaller minimum radii until a reasonable compromise was reached. After much discussion of the various alternatives, the revised standards shown in Table 11-2 were agreed upon.

With these new standards, excellent access was obtained in return for reducing the minimum radius on the main line from 36″ to 30″. Two-foot-wide walk-in aisles were made possible, and wider aisles were achieved in several locations. While a 2-foot-wide aisle makes passage of two persons more of a squeeze than a breeze, universally wider aisles would have meant even further reduction in the minimum radius to the point where the overall character of the railroad would have been changed.

Another important access feature that was achieved was keeping most trackwork within 24″ to 30″ of an aisle. This contributes to ease of construction, maintenance, and operation by keeping important components within easy reach. Pop-up access pits are required in only two locations (the track loops at Hill City and South Omaha/Westport), and these are covered by removable scenic features.

On the O&NW, the difference between 36″ and 30″ curves was further minimized by the use of easements on all curved track. The concept was to help let the equipment, rather than the modeler, do the work and thus add to the enjoyment of the layout over the years.

LOCALE

After the basic shape of the primary trackwork and layout edges had been arrived at, additional sketching soon led to the next compromise. To gain vertical separation between tracks for both operational and scenic purposes, the desired midwestern locale was extended far enough westward to justify some hilly country. While the Midwest isn't really as flat as it is made out to be, tunnels are hard to reconcile with known prototypes.

An imaginary route from Omaha westward was chosen after considering and rejecting such concepts as trees and buildings as the sole means of hiding some of the tracks in congested areas. Hills and tunnels provide a much easier justification for gaining vertical

true in meeting "the" people requirements: designing a railroad that would simultaneously suit the builder, his family, and the club group.

LAYOUT CRITERIA

The next step was to develop a set of standards for the trackwork (Table 11-1) which would permit operation by just about all types of HO scale equipment. At the same time, these standards would permit the layout to challenge the operating capabilities of both the equipment and the operators — a key factor in avoiding boredom.

Note the average train length. It required that steeper grades be built to provide the visible justification for such large power. The design objective then was to match the pulling power of the largest locomotive(s), the average train length, and the ruling grade to the point where smaller locomotives are limited to smaller trains on that grade. Table 11-3 discusses the calculations for determining these grades when located on curves.

separation and for hiding trains from continuous view.

COMPONENT COSTS

Monetary costs were minimized by specifying that track would consist of handlaid ties and rails, including turnouts and crossings. Homebuilt hand-throw mechanisms would be used for turnout control whenever possible. The previously mentioned access considerations allowed locating all but seven turnouts within comfortable reach of an aisle. In the seven locations, including some that were obstructed by proposed scenic features, electrically operated mechanisms were specified. In one of these locations, where vertical access would be restricted in the final stages of the layout, a sectional-track turnout with built-in switch machine was specified despite the much higher initial cost involved. (The price of raw materials, [rails, ties and spikes] for a handlaid turnout amounted to less than 10 percent of a sectional-track equivalent at the time the O&NW was designed.) This was done so that the maintenance or repair could be done by removing the unit as a whole — an important factor in speeding up the process for the critical location at the entrance to the return loop at Westport.

TABLE 11-1
Omaha & North Western design standards — as proposed
Nickel silver rail: code 100 — hidden trackage
83 — main line
70 — mainline sidings, branch line, heavy-use yard trackage
55 — branchline sidings, industries, light-use yard trackage

Trackwork	Primary (1)	Secondary (2)	Other (3)
Minimum radius	36″	32″	24″
Easements (length/width)	18″/½″	18″/½″	16″/⁷⁄₁₆″
Turnouts	No. 6	No. 5	No. 4
Crossovers	No. 6	No. 5	No. 5
Track centers — straight	2″	2″	2″
Track centers — minimum radius	2½″	2⅝″	2¹³⁄₁₆″
Grade — maximum	5%	5%	5%
desired average	2%	2%	2%
switching leads	1%	1%	1%
yards	½%	½%	½%

(1) Primary trackwork consists of the main line, passenger terminal, and the steam engine terminal.
(2) Secondary trackwork consists of mainline passing tracks and the diesel locomotive terminal.
(3) Other trackwork consists principally of the branch line and the industrial spurs.
Average train length: main line, 20 cars; branch line, 10 cars, based on 40-scale-foot cars, each car figured as 6 actual inches in length.

TABLE 11-2
Omaha & North Western design standards — as revised
Nickel silver rail: code 100 — hidden trackage
70 — primary trackage
55 — secondary trackage

Trackwork	Primary (1)	Secondary (2)
Minimum radius	30″	24″
Easements	By eye, using a 36″ length of rail as an aid in determining a natural curve	
Turnouts	No. 6	No. 4
Crossovers	No. 6	No. 5
Track centers — straight	2″	2″
Track centers — curves	2³⁄₁₆″	2³⁄₁₆″
Grades	5% maximum, except 1% maximum in yards	

(1) Primary trackage consists of main line, passenger terminal, main engine terminal, and mainline interchange tracks.
(2) Secondary trackage consists of all other tracks.
Average train length: main line, 16 cars plus engine and caboose.
branch line, 7 cars plus engine and caboose.
(Average car is figured as 6″ long; engine and caboose are figured as 3 cars long for main line and 2½ cars long for branch line.)

Layout at a glance

Name: OMAHA &
NORTH WESTERN
Scale: HO
Space: 17' x 23' x 8'
Location: Basement
Operation: Midwest main line
and branch
Emphasis: Considering all
design factors

Code 100 flexible track was specified for use in those locations where there would be minimal vertical clearance for access. The four spikes to a tie and the free flexing capability of this type of track make it ideal for use in hard-to-reach areas, and especially so in climates where the layout is subjected to large changes in temperature and humidity. The midwestern basement where the O&NW was to be located, and the absence of air conditioning, made this an important consideration.

To help compensate for expansion and contraction, the flexible track is spiked to the roadbed only near the joints, stabilizing the alignment at these critical locations. The middle of each section of flexible track is left unspiked so that it is free to float on the roadbed and absorb expansion and contraction stresses. This may sound a bit odd to those schooled in more conventional techniques, but in practice the free flexing capability allows a very gentle eased curve to form — a curve that is virtually undetectable by eye.

CONTROLS

No other facet of the O&NW required more balancing of requirements than did the electrical control system. This was pretty much expected, given the wide variety of control systems and methods available which were to be matched against the wide spread in the numbers and abilities of the people who would be involved in building, maintaining, and operating the railroad.

One of the first, and more surprising, conclusions reached was that walk-around controls would not be suitable for the O&NW. Restricted aisle widths, lack of aisles which continuously paralleled the likely operating routes, the youth and small stature of the two sons, and the total number of people likely to be present during club operating sessions all argued against walkaround controls. These considerations more than overrode the fact that the O&NW would otherwise be a good railroad on which to use such controls, given the manually thrown turnouts and the car switching operations that were desired.

A mixture of central and local cabs

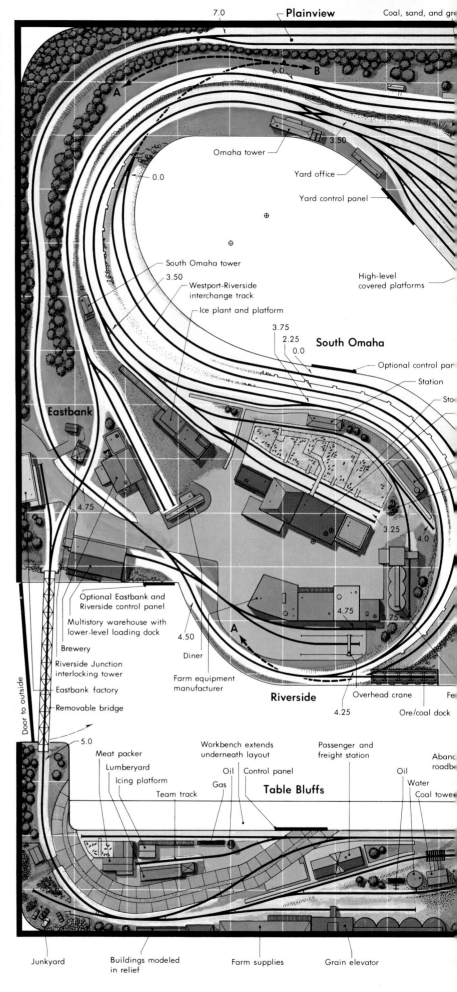

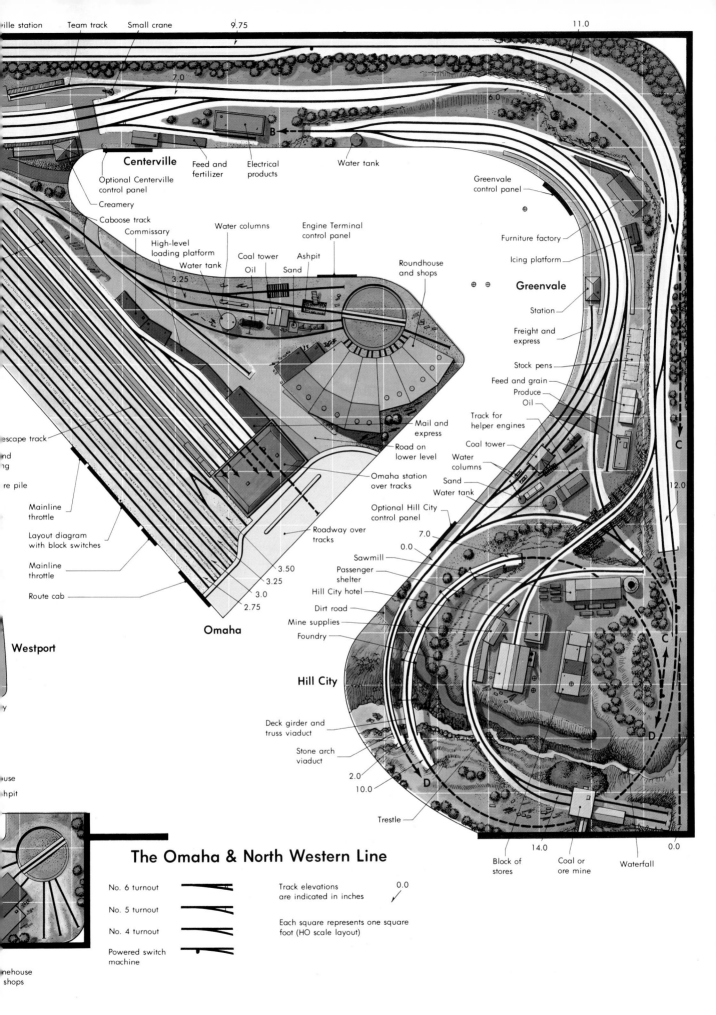

The Omaha & North Western Line

ville station · Team track · Small crane · 9.75 · 11.0

7.0 · 6.0

Centerville · Feed and fertilizer · Electrical products · Water tank · Greenvale control panel

Optional Centerville control panel · Furniture factory

Creamery · Icing platform

Caboose track · Greenvale

Commissary · Station

High-level loading platform · Water columns · Engine Terminal control panel · Freight and express

Water tank · Coal tower · Ashpit · Roundhouse and shops · Stock pens

3.25 · Oil · Sand · Feed and grain · Produce · Oil

Track for helper engines

Mail and express · Coal tower

Road on lower level · Water columns

escape track · Omaha station over tracks · Sand · Water tank

re pile · Optional Hill City control panel · C

Mainline throttle · 7.0 · 12.0

Layout diagram with block switches · Roadway over tracks · 0.0

Mainline throttle · Sawmill

Route cab · Passenger shelter · C

3.50 · Hill City hotel

3.25 · Dirt road

3.0 · Mine supplies

2.75 · Foundry · D

Omaha

Westport · Hill City

Deck girder and truss viaduct

Stone arch viaduct

use · 2.0 · D

hpit · 10.0

Trestle

Block of stores · 14.0 · Coal or ore mine · Waterfall · 0.0

nehouse shops

No. 6 turnout · Track elevations are indicated in inches · 0.0

No. 5 turnout

No. 4 turnout · Each square represents one square foot (HO scale layout)

Powered switch machine

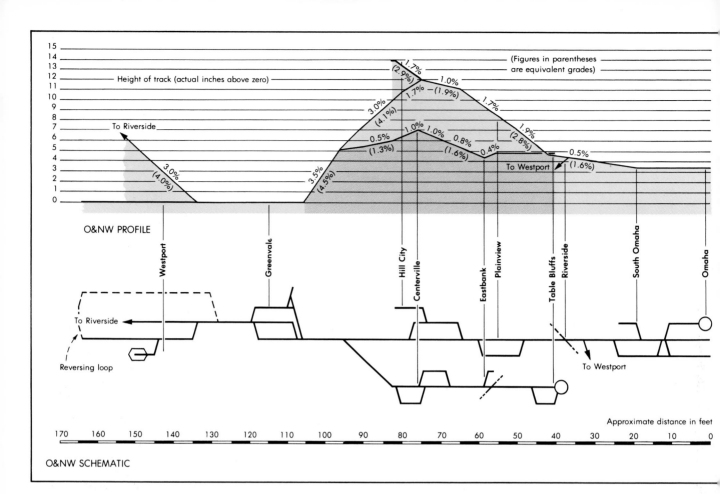

O&NW PROFILE

O&NW SCHEMATIC

was decided upon, with the three central cabs being of two different types. These central cabs were located at the end of the Omaha yard parallel to the yard tracks because there were both space for the operators and a reasonably good view of the entire railroad.

One main cab was a modified version of a route cab with integral cab signals. There were several reasons involved in making this choice. First, the rotary

switch used for power selection ensures that the electrical sections not in use are turned off. This prevents inadvertent operation of other trains running elsewhere on the layout. Second, the integral cab signals provide track occupancy indications for each electrical section as it is connected to the cab. The signals also provide an indication of when to advance the rotary selector switch. Finally, even with all these features, the cost of a route cab is not appreciably different from toggle switch controls on a multisection, multitrain layout. In many cases, route cabs are less costly than conventional cabs.

It was envisioned that the simplicity — from the operator's viewpoint — of route cab control would make it ideal for operators who were either inexperienced or unfamiliar with the layout. To test this belief, a mockup was constructed in advance of the O&NW and the concept was tested by connecting the mockup route cab to sectional track partially simulating the proposed track plan. After a few minutes of instruction, my then 4-year-old son was able to keep a train going on a continuous route without any help, and without interfering with another train's being run from a separate control. The integral signals provided all the information he needed to keep his train under control. Try matching that with any other type of control system!

Two other cabs of conventional de-

sign are located adjacent to the route cab. These cabs each have separate throttles but share a common panel for section-selector toggle switches. The center-off toggles are mounted on a map-type track diagram so that throwing the handle toward a throttle connects the section to that throttle.

Again, this was people consideration for better suiting the control system to on-line switching operations. The map-type track diagram helps orient operators to the track pattern more quickly than schematic diagrams because most modelers have had previous training in map reading. (School geography classes and automobile driving are two examples which precondition modelers to using map-type diagrams.)

The arrangement of the toggle switches makes for easy association of control, throttle, and track location, while the basic mechanics of the toggle switches prevent both controls from being connected to the same section simultaneously. The center-off position is essential to multitrain operation, as this provides a positive off feature for each section.

Control costs were minimized for these throttles by using only one toggle switch for the two cabs. Common-rail wiring was also used; this further minimized costs through reduction of the amount of wire required and by reducing the number of contacts required on rotary and toggle switches to one per pole.

TABLE 11-3

Equivalent grades and grade compensation for curved track*

Radius (inches)	Compensation factor (%)	Radius (inches)	Compensation factor (%)	Radius (inches)	Compensation factor (%)
14	2.3	28	1.1	40	0.8
16	2.0	30	1.1	42	0.8
18	1.8	32	1.0	44	0.7
20	1.6	34	1.0	46	0.7
22	1.5	36	0.9	48	0.7
24	1.3	38	0.8	50	0.6
26	1.2				

Notes:
1. Compensation factor can be computed, for all practical purposes, by using the formula CF = radius of curve in inches divided by 32.
2. Equivalent grade can be determined by the relationship EG = % actual grade + CF.
3. Equivalent grade is defined as grade on curved track which would present the same resistance to a train as an actual grade of the same % on straight track. It is computed for HO scale using car weights equivalent to NMRA Recommended Practice 20.1 (1 ounce + ½ ounce per inch of car length) and car trucks of good quality from various manufacturers. The trucks are *not* of the "super free-rolling" type.
4. The grade compensation factor (CF) can be used in two ways:
   a. By adding the CF to the actual grade, the equivalent grade can be obtained. This can be used after construction to determine engine pulling capacities if a sufficient stretch of straight track is not available for actual measurement.
   b. By subtracting the CF from the equivalent grade desired, the actual grade on a curve can be determined. This can be used in the design and construction stages to establish preselected grades.
*This information is based on empirical data developed by John Allen on the Gorre & Daphetid.

Four local-area control panels were specified, with other possible panel locations indicated if actual operation justifies their construction. These four panels (Table Bluffs, Greenvale, Omaha yard, and Omaha engine terminal) provide local control in areas where there is likely to be considerable switching. At Greenvale, the throttle and reversing switch should be mounted on a cable long enough to allow the operator to reach the manual turnout controls at either end while still holding the throttle.

To simplify control of the wye at Greenvale, contacts on the electrical switch machine were used for automatic routing of power to the tail tracks. The switch machine was required because of poor access resulting from running the Hill City spur in front of the wye turnout.

The Omaha yard panel was built with a track diagram large enough to accommodate switch machine controls in the event that operations justify such an expense. A yard is a focal point for operations under some schemes, so electrically powered switch machines controlled through a diode matrix can help speed up operations and prevent the yard from slowing up the rest of the railroad.

Another control feature derived from the process of matching desires with feasibilities was the decision to have the mainline/branchline crossing insulated and wired so that a separate electrical control switch would be required. This switch serves to interlock the two routes by preventing both from being powered simultaneously. Although the additional switch is somewhat inconvenient when experienced operators are running trains, it does help prevent broadside collisions when less experienced operators, such as the two young sons, are at the controls. An additional set of contacts on the same control switch is used to set trackside signals that indicate which route is selected and powered.

One unplanned feature of the control system turned up serendipitously while reviewing the overall plan. By preselecting a route in one of the toggle-switch cabs and setting the appropriate throttle and reversing switch to run a train at moderate speed, an acceptable form of walkaround control for use during one-man operation can be achieved. The lone operator can set up the main cab and then walk to one of the local-area cabs where he can gain control of the train when it reaches the local electrical section. The operator can then conduct switching operations using the local cab and, when finished, turn control back to the main cab while he walks on to the next location.

CONSTRUCTION STAGES

While a yard can be a focal point for

operations, in the early stages of a layout it is more likely to be a set of dead storage tracks with little operating potential. To gain and maintain interest during these early stages, trackwork should be started at the branchline terminal of Table Bluffs. The trackwork at Table Bluffs is relatively easy to build and to wire — an important consideration in getting part of the layout in operation as soon as is possible. Since the workbench is located underneath this area, the track is also very convenient for testing equipment as it is built or repaired.

Other reasons for starting at Table Bluffs are the plentiful opportunities for spotting cars and making other

switching moves. New or inexperienced operators will find many ways to learn and practice these operations, while older hands will find themselves challenged by the track layout, which requires use of either the turntable or two locomotives in order to switch all of the industries.

From Table Bluffs, tracklaying crews should advance along the branch line and then the main line in stages as are shown in Fig. 11-1. The next area to be completed would be Centerville, which would provide a short point-to-point operation with some switching at both ends.

Although Centerville's full trackwork is quite flexible, operation can be made

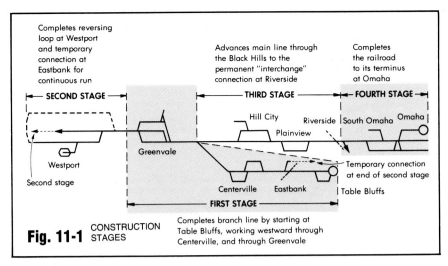

Fig. 11-1 CONSTRUCTION STAGES

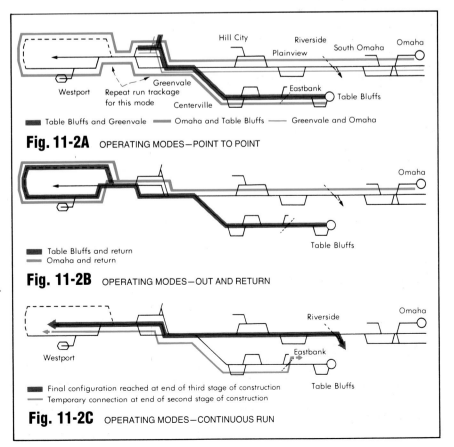

Fig. 11-2A OPERATING MODES—POINT TO POINT

Fig. 11-2B OPERATING MODES—OUT AND RETURN

Fig. 11-2C OPERATING MODES—CONTINUOUS RUN

deceptively difficult by throwing in a few tricks. First, a typical prototypic feature is added in the form of a string of cars in dead storage on the northeastern portion of the lap siding. Then the trains are made just a bit longer than capacity of the other siding, and the operator is confronted with several extra moves in order to switch all of the industries. Note that these conditions reinforce the emphasis on operating Centerville from the aisle at the western end. Turnouts were purposely laid out in this manner so that the operator can avoid the long walk (or need for assistance) that would be required for operating the turnout at the eastern end.

From Centerville, the track crews go on to the ruling grade on the loop descending into Greenvale. Although both the main line and the branch line will eventually share the track on the loop, only the branchline trains will traverse the grade at this point in the construction. The wye and the other trackage at Greenvale make it possible for branchline trains to run in full point-to-point fashion with the locomotives being turned at each end of the run. The long tail of the wye is provided to simulate an interchange with a connecting railroad.

The next stage of construction consists of the trackwork from Greenvale through Westport, including the return loop and interchange track at the latter location. The interchange track climbs up to what will eventually be Riverside, but for the moment it is temporarily connected to the industrial spur at Eastbank. This provides a route for continuous running.

The return loop at Westport was designed for counterclockwise operation in order to facilitate switching of the car ferry and the interchange track. These destinations provide both ample capacity and logical routing for all types of cars and loads at this end-of-the-line location.

After Westport has been completed, track construction crews return to the Black Hills to commence work on the main line up to Hill City. Work then progresses through Plainview and on to Riverside, where the temporary connection between the interchange track and Eastbank is broken and the permanent mainline connection is made.

At this stage in the construction, the branch line and the main line can be operated as separate entities. The branch can be operated point to point between Table Bluffs and Greenvale, while the main can be operated as a continuous loop. One mainline train in each direction could be used in this scheme, and since the return loop at Westport wouldn't be needed for reversing it could be used as an interchange track.

The final stage of construction advances the trackwork to the Omaha terminal and includes the heavily industrialized area of South Omaha. The two tracks between Omaha and South Omaha create the flexibility needed for multitrain and multiperson operation. Both tracks can be used as leads for switching either the passenger or the freight yard and as passing tracks for trains entering or departing the terminal. The secondary track also functions as a lead for switching South Omaha without interfering with traffic to and from Omaha.

At Omaha, passenger and freight facilities exist side by side with a common engine escape track between the respective arrival tracks. The engine terminal probably has more engine storage space than is strictly required, but model railroads tend to have more motive power than is required, too. Freight yards are located nearer the table edge on the presumption that there will be more switching of freight than passenger cars and therefore the freight cars should be in a position to be seen or adjusted easier.

This proposed construction sequence is definitely not prototypic, as any railroad traversing the imaginary route in real life would proceed in almost directly opposite fashion. The reasons for the proposed model construction stages are, once more, the people considerations — gaining and maintaining the interest of the modelers concerned by providing the maximum operating possibilities in a rapid and logical sequence.

OPERATION

The O&NW has many different operating possibilities, as shown in fig. 11-2. Engine turning facilities are located at Table Bluffs, Greenvale, and Omaha for use in conjunction with point-to-point operations, while a return loop at Westport adds another method of turning for out-and-back operation of entire trains. The interchange track from Westport to Eastbank/Riverside provides a continuous route for breaking in equipment, display running for casual visitors, and, not the least important, for use by the two young sons of the builder.

The suggested industries are well diversified and they provide suitable destinations for almost every type of car and load imaginable. The inclusion of all-purpose destinations such as team tracks, interchange tracks, and the car ferry provides ample and varied routing patterns for any oddball cars that would otherwise require and monopolize spurs at unique industries. At the same time, these same tracks provide ample and logical destinations for regular cars without using much additional space.

Table 11-4 provides a list of suggested industries, loads, and car types for each area on the O&NW. The overall emphasis is on industries whose loads would provide a car mix suggestive of the Midwest. General cargo cars, such as boxcars, would predominate over more specialized cars, such as hoppers. A color-coded car routing system, Table 11-5, was proposed to govern the movements of individual cars. Color coding has proved to be a means of rapidly conveying information on car

TABLE 11-4
Car destinations

Area	Industry/Destination	Loads	Car types*
Table Bluffs	Enginehouse	Machinery, supplies	F, B
	Engine service tracks	Coal, oil, ashes, sand	H, T, G
	Freight station	Express, general cargo	B, R, F, X
	Grain elevator	Grain	CH, B
	Farm Supply	Farm supplies	B
	Team track	General cargo	B, F, G, R
	Lumberyard	Wood	B, F
	Fuel, Oil & Gas	Petroleum products	T
	Ice	Ice	R
	Meat packer	Animals, meat products	S, R
Eastbank	Factory	General cargo	B
	Brewery	Grain, booze, supplies, fuel	CH, B, R, T, H
	Team track	General cargo	B, F, G, R
Centerville	Electrical mfr.	Supplies, products	B
	Feed & Fertilizer	Feed, fertilizer	B, CH, T
	Creamery	Milk products	R
	Coal, Sand & Gravel	Coal, sand, gravel	H, G
	Team track	General cargo	B, F, G. R
	Station	Express	X
Greenvale	Engine service tracks	Coal, oil, ashes, sand	H, T, G
	Station	Express	X
	Interchange	All	All
	Produce	Produce	R
	Feed & Grain	Feeds, grain	CH, B
	Stock pens	Animals	S
	Ice	Ice	R
	Furniture factory	Furniture, wood	B, F
Westport	Interchange	All	All
	Car ferry	All	All
Hill City	Sawmill	Logs, lumber	B, F
	Foundry	Metal products	G, F, H
	Mine Supplies	Mine supplies	B, F, G
	Mine	Minerals	H, O, G
Riverside	Warehouse	General cargo	B
	Farm equipment mfr.	Supplies, farm equip.	B, F, G
	Ore/coal dock	Minerals	O, H
	Interchange	All	All
South Omaha	Stock pens	Animals	S
	Hides & Rendering	Hides, tallow	B, T
	Manure pile	Fertilizer	G
	Feed	Grain, feed	CH, B
	Meat packer	Meat products	R
	Ice	Ice	R
Omaha	Freight yard	All	All
	Commissary	Food	B, R
	Mail & Express	Mail, express	X, B
	Engine service tracks	Coal, oil, ashes, sand	H, T, G
	Engine shops	Machinery, supplies	F, B

*B, boxcar; CH, covered hopper car; F, flatcar; G, gondola car; H, hopper car; O, ore car; R, refrigerator car; S, stockcar; T, tank car; X, express car.

TABLE 11-5
Omaha & North Western area color codes

Area	Color	Association factor
Omaha	Red	Almost everyone in the Midwest knows that Nebraska is the Big Red.
South Omaha	Yellow	Yellow is near to red in the color spectrum (but not too near to cause confusion) and South Omaha is near to Omaha.
Riverside	Blue	The blues began, and became famous in, cities by the river (Saint Louis Blues, Kansas City Blues, etc.).
Plainview	None	There's nothing to be seen or done here.
Hill City	Black	The real Hill City is near the real Black Hills.
Greenvale	Green	Down in the valley, the vegetation is thicker; and, besides, the color is in the area name.
Westport	Orange	The orange sun sets in the West.
Centerville	White	A plain midwestern plains town with a plain color.
Eastbank	Brown and white	Partly near Centerville and partly near Table Bluffs, the color is partly part of each.
Table Bluffs	Brown	That's the color of tables and bluffs.

destinations — an important consideration on a layout with diverse people requirements.

Operation on the O&NW is envisioned as using a two-man crew for each train, the crew being composed of an engineer and a conductor. The engineer would be responsible for keeping the schedule and for following the hand signals of the conductor during switching operations. Making the engineer responsible for keeping the schedule resulted from the decision to use central cabs. Since the engineers are all physically grouped together, it is easy for them to agree on the location of meets not specified in the timetable.

The conductors can either follow one train, throwing turnouts as required and deciding on the switching moves to be made, or they can stay in one general area, directing all movements in that area. The former method seems preferable for the variety involved, but the latter might be required if too many people are present to permit free movement in the aisles.

Operation of the completed O&NW would involve mainline trains running from Omaha to Westport and return. Local freights would make set-outs and pickups at the industries along the way, while through freights could carry cars destined for the interchanges at Greenvale and Westport. Naturally, passenger trains could be interspersed among the freights.

On the branch line, smaller and older locomotives would meander between Table Bluffs and Greenvale, where the branchline trains would make connections with the mainline trains. Mixed trains or an occasional doodlebug would be appropriate accommodation for passengers along the branch.

Switch engines would be stationed at Omaha and Greenvale. The Omaha switcher(s) would handle traffic from South Omaha, while the Greenvale switcher would be of a type powerful enough to double as a helper for trains climbing the ruling grade into the Black Hills. A separate helper could also be stationed at Greenvale, but things might get a little congested when both main and branch trains are present at the same time as two local engines.

Local switching at Table Bluffs would be performed by whatever branchline power happened to be available at the time, including the aforementioned doodlebug. Generally, one inbound and one outbound locomotive would be sufficient power for Table Bluffs. The number of cars associated with an inbound and an outbound train present at the same time should be sufficient for the Table Bluffs operator's headache, too.

PLANS AND PLANNING

To me, there is a considerable differ-

A Chicago & North Western diesel freight interrupts the quiet of a barren Nebraska plain. One of the desired features of this track plan was a midwestern setting; this diesel has found a typical one.

ence between a *track* plan and a *layout* plan. A track plan deals with just the track and perhaps the scenery, and can result in anything from a toy train loop to a model railroad. A layout plan is aimed at obtaining a model railroad by considering all of the factors involved and integrating them into a whole. Such a plan necessarily incorporates a track plan as part of the overall scheme.

This by no means implies that any layout plan is perfect. There is a limit to what can be considered during the design process, and it is doubtful that any layout ever ends up exactly as it was planned. There are just too many things that come to light as the railroad is operated in different manners,

and there are continually new ideas coming to the fore in this wonderful hobby. The key is to devote some time to a careful and reasoned layout plan, and then remain flexible as the plan is constructed and the railroad matures.

In designing the O&NW, the prime emphasis was on meeting the people requirements while considering such other features as track standards, access, imaginary locale, component costs, control system construction stages, and operation as a model railroad. The process of considering these and arriving at suitable compromises is the story of the Omaha & North Western — a plan for all reasons.

In the 1960s the Reader RR became popular with railfans looking for one last place to ride behind steam. Reader is pronounced "reeder," which would be obvious, except that we had that eastern railroad , the Reading, which was pronounced "redding."

READER RAILROAD

An HO layout that shares its living quarters with the family car

Sometimes you have a big train room, but can't use much of it for a model railroad. This stems from a gross architectural myth holding that most houses should have a big room attached with an extra-large door, large enough for a car or two to go through. The myth further holds that this room should be devoted to the storage of automobiles, garden implements, and other assorted junk — and that this space be identified as the "garage," rather than the train room.

My friend and fellow track planner Rick Mugele realizes the absurdity of this myth, but was willing to compromise in designing this HO layout so that the train room could be shared with automobiles.

Two features make this coexistence feasible. Most of the layout is to be built on a narrow shelf projecting from the walls of the garage — er, train room. Furthermore, these shelves will be mounted high enough to clear opened car doors.

The highest point on the layout, Waterloo, should still be within easy reach. If not, the modeler could stand on a

step stool or a low bench to attain a comfortable working position.

The leg of the Waterloo wye and the reversing loop at the north end of the Missouri Pacific will project into the automobile space, but they are mounted on hinged, swing-down sections constructed as shown on page 51.

THE PROTOTYPE

The Reader RR, located in the southwest corner of Arkansas, was assembled from a network of logging lines started in 1913. Formal incorporation took place in 1925 and was spurred by the discovery of oil and the construction of the Berry Oil refinery in Waterloo.

The local crude was so dense — some accounts say 45 percent asphalt — that it could be pumped only while heated. A heated pipeline was impractical, so the oil had to be refined locally, and the

products shipped by rail. This accounted for the Reader surviving until 1973, when the refinery was closed. The refinery also accounted for the line being steam-powered for its entire life, as engine fuel was purchased directly from the refinery's tanks.

The Reader ran through woods and marshes, paralleling 15-foot-wide Caney Creek for most of its length. There were 126 trestles on the line, 7 of which crossed the creek, while the others crossed associated ponds, ditches, and drainage canals. The watery setting abounded with beavers and other wildlife. During deer season, trains stopped along the right-of-way to take hunters to and from otherwise inaccessible stands.

The rail was light and the roadbed rough — so rough that the engine bells rang themselves on the worst sections of track. Obviously the trains ran slow.

The frequency with which the trains ran varied between three times and once a week, depending on economic conditions. The line's Baldwin-built Prairies (Nos. 11 and 108) and Consolidation (No. 1702) hauled mostly short trains of 12 to 14 tank cars between the Missouri Pacific interchange at Reader and the refinery at Waterloo.

The remaining 20 percent of the freight traffic consisted of boxcars, gondolas, and flats going to and from a planing mill, crosstie plants, and temporary logging operations in the woods.

These steam locomotives attracted more and more visitors as mainline railroads switched to diesel power. Seeing the potential for some extra revenue, the line's president, Thomas W. M. Long, decided to institute passenger service in 1963. "Mr. Tom," as he was widely known, bought two pas-

Roy W. Turner

Pogo and his friends from the swamp would have felt right at home living alongside the Reader RR. Here engine no. 11 stops to take on water, not — as you might guess — from the tank, but directly from the bayou using a hose. Meanwhile, the brakeman sees if the fish are biting.

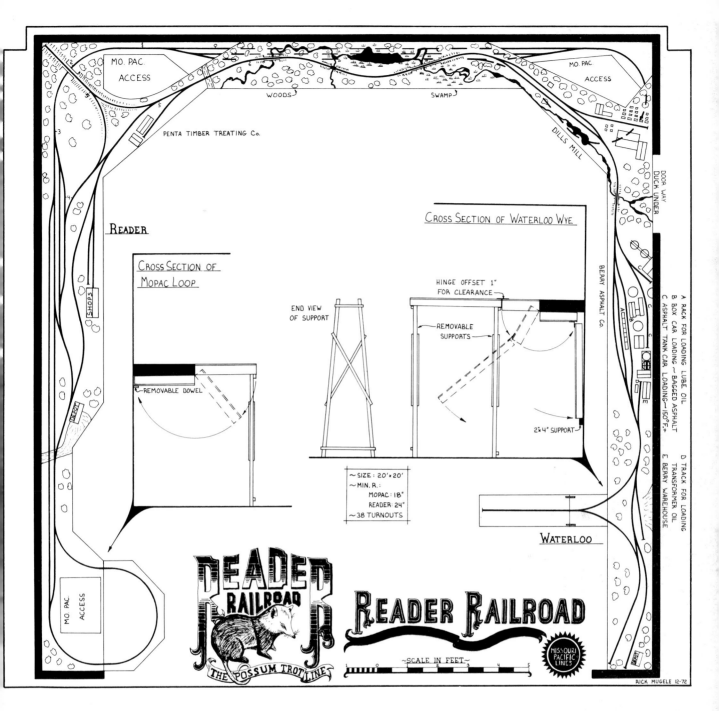

MO. PAC. ACCESS

WOODS

SWAMP

MO. PAC. ACCESS

PENTA TIMBER TREATING Co.

DILLS MILL

READER

DOOR WAY DUCK UNDER

CROSS SECTION OF WATERLOO WYE

HINGE OFFSET 1" FOR CLEARANCE

CROSS SECTION OF MOPAC LOOP

REMOVABLE SUPPORTS

BERRY ASPHALT Co.

END VIEW OF SUPPORT

SHOPS

REMOVABLE DOWEL

2×4" SUPPORT

DEPOT

~ SIZE : 20'×20'
~ MIN. R. :
 MOPAC : 18"
 READER : 24"
~ 38 TURNOUTS

WATERLOO

A RACK FOR LOADING LUBE OIL
B BOX CAR LOADING ~ BAGGED ASPHALT
C ASPHALT TANK CAR LOADING~150°F.+
D TRACK FOR LOADING TRANSFORMER OIL
E BERRY WAREHOUSE

MO. PAC. ACCESS

READER RAILROAD

THE POSSUM TROT LINE

READER RAILROAD

MISSOURI PACIFIC LINES

~SCALE IN FEET~

DEPOT

RICK MUGELE 12-72

Layout at a glance

Name: READER RAILROAD
Scale: HO
Space: 20' x 20' x 8'
Location: Garage
Operation: Simple mainline and short line
Emphasis: Dual-purpose layout space

senger cars: a parlor car and a baggage-coach combination.

The Reader then offered a mixed train service rather than a tourist operation, though amenities were added to accommodate passengers while the freight work was being done. Unfortunately, the remote location of the Reader precluded attempts to preserve it as a purely tourist line.

OPERATION

The years from 1963 to 1972 offer the best possibilities for a model railroad, and that's the period this layout is designed to capture. By that time the Missouri Pacific was entirely dieselized and running relatively modern, fast freights. By contrast, the Reader RR remained 100 percent steam-powered and was running short, slow trains through the backwoods.

Rick took this mechanical diversity into account in choosing the curve minimums. The MoPac diesels can negotiate tight curves, permitting an 18" radius to be used on the end loops. The Reader, the focus of the layout, uses 24"-radius curves to make the steam locomotives and passenger cars look better in operation.

Model operations could closely parallel those on the real Reader. The MoPac freights would appear on stage, drop off cars for the short line at the Reader interchange, then continue on until reaching the hidden storage tracks.

One of the Reader's steam engines would then move out and couple to the freight cars. The passenger cars would be tacked on at the tail, and the mixed train would head toward Waterloo, switching as required along the route. At Waterloo, the passenger cars would be uncoupled and spotted at the depot before the oil refinery was switched. With the refinery work complete, the passenger cars would be coupled back on and the train would return to Reader.

Richard J. Cook photo

A Baltimore and Ohio diesel freight crosses the Allegheny River in Pennsylvania around 1954. The fate of the B&O was instrumental in setting up the events which served as the inspiration for the Mahoning Creek RR.

THE MAHONING CREEK and THE BRADFORD, RIDGWAY & PUNXSUTAWNEY

Two alternatives for a spacious room

Although space for model railroads is usually limited, that doesn't mean spacious layout rooms can't be found. And when they are, you'll discover that design options increase correspondingly. One way to make the most out of these increased options is to draw a number of different layouts suitable for the space available. The Mahoning Creek (MC) and the Bradford, Ridgway & Punxsutawney (BR&P) are two examples of layouts created this way.

These two railroads fit into the same 22' x 25' space. They represent the same geographical area but reflect different themes — multiple branch lines for the MC, heavy-duty single-track mainline railroading for the BR&P. The following track criteria applied to both: minimum radii of 30" on the main and 24" on branch or industrial trackage; No. 6 turnouts leading off the main and No. 4 elsewhere; and 3 percent maximum grades except on industrial spurs.

Few physical obstacles interfered with layout construction. An insulated chimney pipe ran up through the room, but the space between the chimney and the wall was usable for model railroad purposes. Access between the two doorways located on opposite sides of the room had to be maintained. One entry had a short flight of stairs leading up into the room, so it could be permanently bridged by tracks if they were at least 56" above the floor. The other entry also could be spanned by tracks, but they had to be removed between operating sessions.

THE SETTING

Both railroads are set in the area around Punxsutawney, Pennsylvania, a town located 60 miles northeast of Pittsburgh. The town is perhaps best known for Punxsutawney Phil, the groundhog who checks his shadow every February 2nd to predict the weather for the following six weeks. If Phil left his hole more often, he'd find a good deal of farming and coal mining going on in the surrounding countryside.

And if Phil were interested in railroads, he would revel in the variety of lines that laced the territory. Almost every valley and vale has seen a track at one time or another. The first railroad to reach this area was the Brockwayville & Punxsutawney, which arrived in the early 1880s. One hundred years later the Chessie System still maintained a division point in Punxsutawney while lines of Conrail and the Pittsburg & Shawmut reached nearby.

The Brockwayville & Punxsutawney has evolved into the Buffalo & Pittsburgh. The original B&P became part of the Buffalo, Rochester & Pittsburgh, which in turn was absorbed by the Baltimore & Ohio in the 1930s. The B&O was later folded into the Chessie System, and the lines from Pittsburgh to Buffalo and Rochester were sold off in the '80s.

Coal mines just outside town were once reached by the extreme south end of the Buffalo & Susquehanna. Abandoned right-of-way fragments of the B&S were later used by the Clearfield & Jefferson, which eventually became the Bellwood Branch of the Pennsylvania RR. The Bellwood Branch lasted through the Penn Central merger and into Conrail before it was pulled up.

The other part of the PC, the New York Central, also extended into the Punxsutawney area at one time. A few miles of spur to a coal mine were gained by trackage rights over the C&J. These rights were actually held by the Canoe Creek RR, an offshoot of the NYC's Beach Creek RR subsidiary. Other short lines, branch lines, and spurs served the numerous coal mines and related industries — coke ovens, lumbering (for mine timbers), scrap yards — in the surrounding area.

THE MAHONING CREEK RAILROAD

The inspiration for the MC was the many branches and short lines that served the Punxsutawney area. These all had been absorbed into the three major lines — B&O, PRR, and NYC — before the start of World War Two. After the war, economic conditions forced these three lines into the Chessie and Conrail systems, which had the con-

Many industries are located in the valleys along the former BR&P line of the Chessie System. The tree-covered hills can be readily duplicated as a model railroad backdrop.

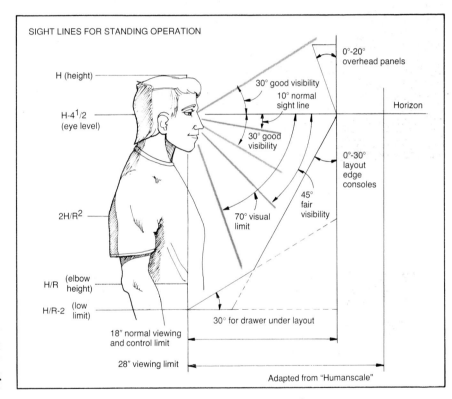

verse effect of freeing some of the former short lines and branches for independent operation.

In theory, the Mahoning Creek railroad was formed to operate these lines. The MC started with a motley collection of small steamers saved from scrap. Eventually, a few secondhand industrial diesels were added. Some of these engines still see use for contracted industrial switching, but the bulk of the MC motive power now consists of first-generation Geeps.

Headquartered in Punxsutawney, the MC interchanges traffic with the B&O. Switching in Riker yard and the former

city branch has been contracted to the MC. Two important MC routes share trackage from Cloe to Creekside Junction. The Shelocta line handles unit trains of hoppers to the power plant, while the Indiana Branch serves the carload industries remaining to the south.

Trackage rights over the B&O allow the MC to reach its isolated Falls Creek Branch. The Falls Creek Branch serves two major industries, the glass plant at Brockway and the car shops at Dubois. Fact meets fiction at these car shops. The real BR&P had an extensive complex at Dubois, where much of its steam locomotive roster was built. An independent car repair firm now uses what buildings remain in the complex. In the model world, the Dubois car shops are another operation of the ingenious MC. Aside from the railroad traffic generated, the shops provide excellent justification for operating and displaying equipment that doesn't fit the overall layout theme.

The abridged B&O trackage between Punxsutawney and the hidden reversing loop under Brockway represent mainline operation. At least one pair of sizable unit trains can be operated on the B&O by means of the empty/load connection between Nora Mine and the Shelocta Power Plant. The Cloe-Creekside Junction siding is also long enough to hold one of these unit hopper trains, adding more operating flexibility.

DESIGN DETAILS

The MC is a walk-in walkalong combination that requires operators to move with their trains. A double-faced backdrop reaching above eye level on the center peninsula visually divides the room into separate parts, further enhancing the feeling of being associated with a particular train. Control by tethered throttles would be impractical for this aisle arrangement, so push-button control posts or plug-in throttles would be best. Carrier control would add a lot of realism if the receivers could be fitted into the small engines.

Behind-the-backdrop openings at Cloe and Brockway provide access to areas not easily reached from the operating aisles. The curved wye turnout at Cloe is hidden under the scenery, but located close to the aisle edge at Shelocta for access. A small section of removable scenery above this turnout would help increase the ease of access.

The other hidden turnouts are on the B&O reverse loop under Brockway. Access could be provided from underneath if the scenery were made high enough. A better idea would be to take advantage of the woods to conceal a large removable scenery section permitting top access.

Phased construction is desirable on a layout as large as the MC. Construction first starts at Punxsutawney so that yard and industry switching operations can commence as soon as track is laid. This is followed by the B&O main line from Cloe to the reversing loop to provide out-and-back operation. The Falls Creek Branch is next, completing the work on that side of the room as well as providing industries to be switched at the far end of the line.

Up to now, the center of the room has remained free for lumber handling and cutting, but this space is lost once construction of the Indiana Branch is

started. The final segment of the MC to be constructed is the Shelocta line and the empty/load connection back to the B&O through Nora Mine.

THE BRADFORD, RIDGWAY & PUNXSUTAWNEY

Mainline operation is the theme of the BRP. Town names and industries reflect those on the real Buffalo, Rochester & Pittsburgh, but no attempt is made to replicate specific prototype scenes. The model BRP is set in the steam-to-diesel transition era to justify operation of a wide variety of motive power and rolling stock. The large number of railroad-served industries reflects this era, but also provides a switching counterpoint to run-through operations for mainline trains.

Riker Yard is the focus of operations. This division point handles virtually every freight train on the BRP, adding and subtracting cars as required by their waybills. Yard tracks are designated by primary function to help organize this work. The engine terminal at Riker is abbreviated, but the 15″ turntable will handle good-sized locomotives. It is the only turning facility on the railroad.

The main line is a continuous single track running twice around the room. Passing sidings provide a multi-train operating capacity. The hidden spiral between the Johnsonburg paper mill and Dubois is the base for a PRR train that interchanges cars with the BRP both places. A 30′-long section of hidden double track between Bradford and Punxsutawney serves as a linear staging area. This represents prototype destinations of Butler at the south (Punxsutawney) end of the prototype and Salamanca at the north (Bradford) end.

SPECIAL CONSIDERATIONS

Unique to the BRP are the layout-to-ceiling backdrops on the two peninsulas. These provide a stunning effect, creating the illusion that the railroad runs through a series of connected valleys. Since no more than a third of the layout is visible from any one view-

Layout at a glance

Name: MAHONING CREEK; BRADFORD, RIDGWAY & PUNXSUTAWNEY
Scale: HO
Space: 24' x 25' x 8'
Location: Built in layout room
Operation: Branch line vs. main line
Emphasis: Alternatives with same prototypes

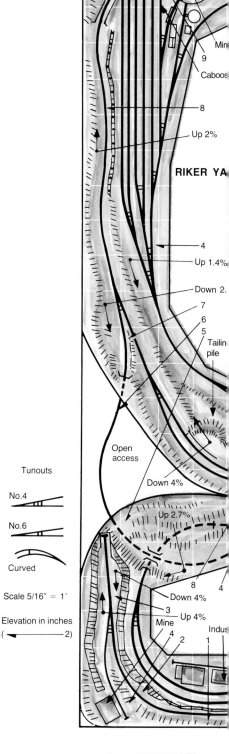

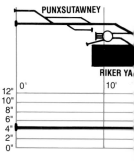

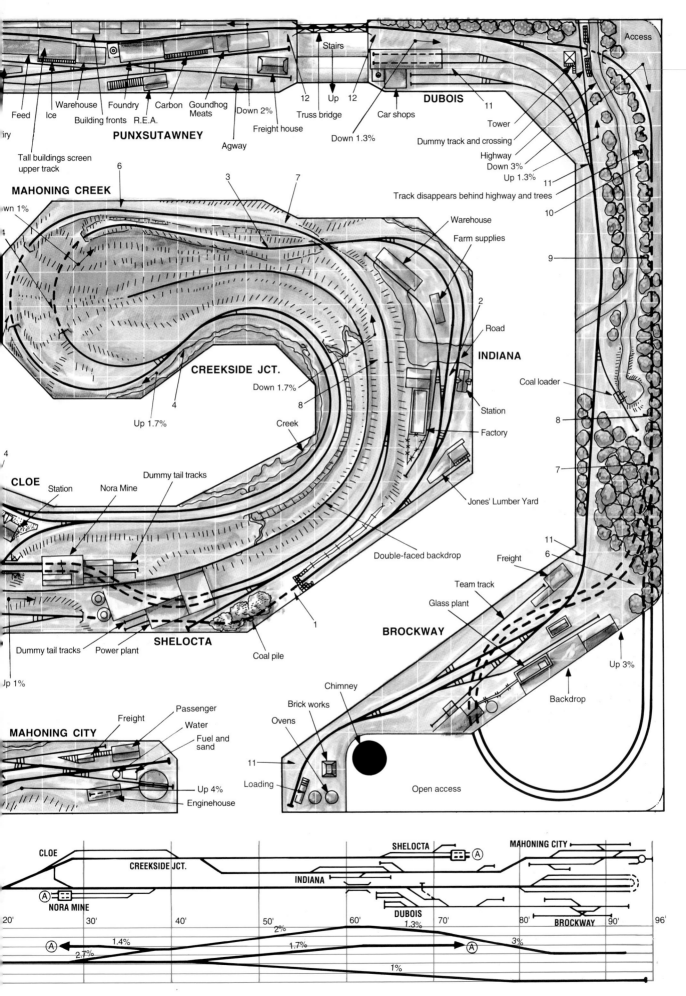

PUNXSUTAWNEY

Feed
Ice
Warehouse
Building fronts
Foundry
R.E.A.
Carbon
Goundhog Meats
Agway
Down 2%
Freight house
Stairs
12 Up 12
Truss bridge
Down 1.3%
Car shops
DUBOIS
11
Tower
Dummy track and crossing
Highway
Down 3%
Up 1.3%
11
Access
10
Track disappears behind highway and trees

Tall buildings screen upper track

MAHONING CREEK
6
3
7
wn 1%

Warehouse
Farm supplies
9
2
Road
INDIANA
Station
Factory
Coal loader
8
7

CREEKSIDE JCT.
Down 1.7%
8
Up 1.7%
Creek
4

CLOE
Station
Nora Mine
Dummy tail tracks
Double-faced backdrop
Jones' Lumber Yard
Freight
11
6
Team track
Glass plant

Dummy tail tracks
Power plant
SHELOCTA
Coal pile
1
BROCKWAY
Up 3%
Backdrop

Up 1%

MAHONING CITY
Freight
Passenger
Water
Fuel and sand
Up 4%
Enginehouse
Chimney
Brick works
Ovens
Loading
11
Open access

CLOE
CREEKSIDE JCT.
SHELOCTA
MAHONING CITY
INDIANA
NORA MINE
DUBOIS
BROCKWAY

20'   30'   40'   50'   60'   70'   80'   90'   96'
1.3%
2%
1.4%
1.7%
3%
2.7%
1%

point, the layout room also seems vastly increased in size.

BREATHING ROOM

Installing layout-to-ceiling backdrops like those on the BRP can significantly affect air circulation patterns. Heat and humidity generated by the operators have to be carried away to keep working conditions comfortable. Fortunately, the BRP had an attic access hatch in the ceiling near the chimney pipe. An exhaust fan running at low speed provides the necessary draft to keep air moving. Circulation control is obtained by closing the door nearest the fan.

On another layout using similar high internal backdrops, the air flow problem was solved by leaving a 4"-6" space between the top of the backdrops and the ceiling. The success of this method seemed related to the location of the air intake and exhaust vents already existing in the basement layout room.

PEOPLE VS. CONTROLS

The ease with which people can move around in the operating aisle must also be considered. The 3'-wide aisles of the BRP are adequate, but not great, for multi-person operation. This is true even of places like Riker where there was room to widen the aisles slightly. With walkalong design, busy locations for trains become busy locations for people; therefore, control panels should not protrude too far into already tight aisle space.

Model railroaders have devised many ways to mount control panels so they don't take up too much space in the operating aisle. These include panels that slide under the layout on rollers, panels recessed into the layout edge, and panels mounted above the layout. An almost infinite variety of arrangements is possible depending on the viewing and operating space available, the construction of the layout and benchwork, and the preferences of the builder. The illustration on page 53 shows some of the considerations for achieving ergonomically desirable panel viewing angles.

There are other visual considerations for building control panels. Displayed information should be legible and large enough to be easily read. Lettering and line diagrams should have a high contrast with the background color and should not be obscured by controls. Color coding should be used for emphasis, but the use of too many colors should be avoided.

Furthermore, electrical controls should be within easy reach. Frequently operated controls should operate freely, but not so freely that accidental operation is likely. Toggle switches, in particular, can be snagged by loose clothing and may require protective guards. Controls having

different functions should be differentiated by varying their size and shape.

Push buttons have a natural operating motion and are well suited for rapid control inputs. One place where such inputs might be required on a model railroad is for yard switching. Route control using one push button per track to line up all turnouts simplifies operation at the relatively modest cost of added wiring complexity.

All controls should give feedback to the operator. Control handle positions or contact click sounds are two examples of such feedback. Controls that do not have an inherent feedback (some push buttons) should have an external signal added. Feedback of the control *function* should also be provided, i.e., an indication that operation of the control provided the desired result.

Our eyes provide rapid feedback for three of the four control functions necessary in model railroading: speed, direction, and turnout position. The other necessary control function is connecting the propulsion power to the correct train. When you can't see for yourself, as on long stretches of hidden track, you'll need alternative signals. These can take the form of lights on the control panel or of model signals on the layout.

Layout signals can also be used to convey some propulsion power information by simulating prototypic approach lighting. Instead of the signal lights coming on when a train is approaching the signal block, the model signals can be wired so that they light when propulsion power is applied to the track block.

A signal system providing feedback information would be useful on the BRP, although not absolutely required. The twists and turns in the operating aisle keep sighting distances short, particularly when the trains make 180-degree turns around the ends of the two peninsulas. Feedback, either from a signal system or the modern practice of using radio information, is needed before sending trains around the bend.

Operators should always stay ahead of their trains. This way they can make sure the track ahead is clear, the turnouts are set correctly, and their operations are coordinated with those of other operators. Obtaining feedback information this very human way can save operators the costs and complexities of mechanical and electrical systems.

THE CHOICE

The differing themes of the MC and BRP reinforce the point made at the beginning of this chapter: When the layout space is large, alternative designs should be drawn as an aid to making informed choices about a prospective model empire. The final choice will be a matter of preference and may even include elements of several plans.

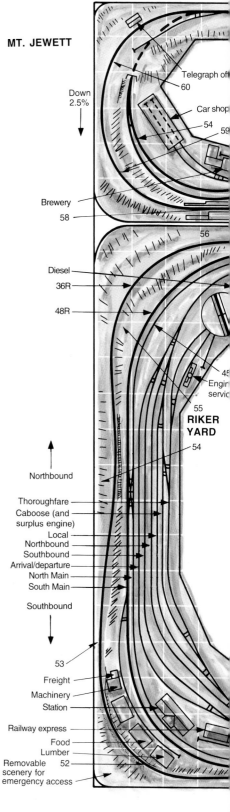

MT. JEWETT

Down 2.5%

Telegraph office 60

Car shop 54 59

Brewery 58

56

Diesel 36R

48R

48 Engine service

55 RIKER YARD

54

Northbound

Thoroughfare
Caboose (and surplus engine)
Local
Northbound
Southbound
Arrival/departure
North Main
South Main

Southbound

53

Freight
Machinery
Station
Railway express
Food
Lumber 52
Removable scenery for emergency access

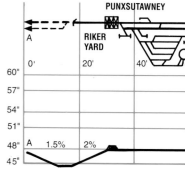

PUNXSUTAWNEY

A

RIKER YARD

A

0'   20'   40'

60"
57"
54"
51"
48" A   1.5%   2%
45"

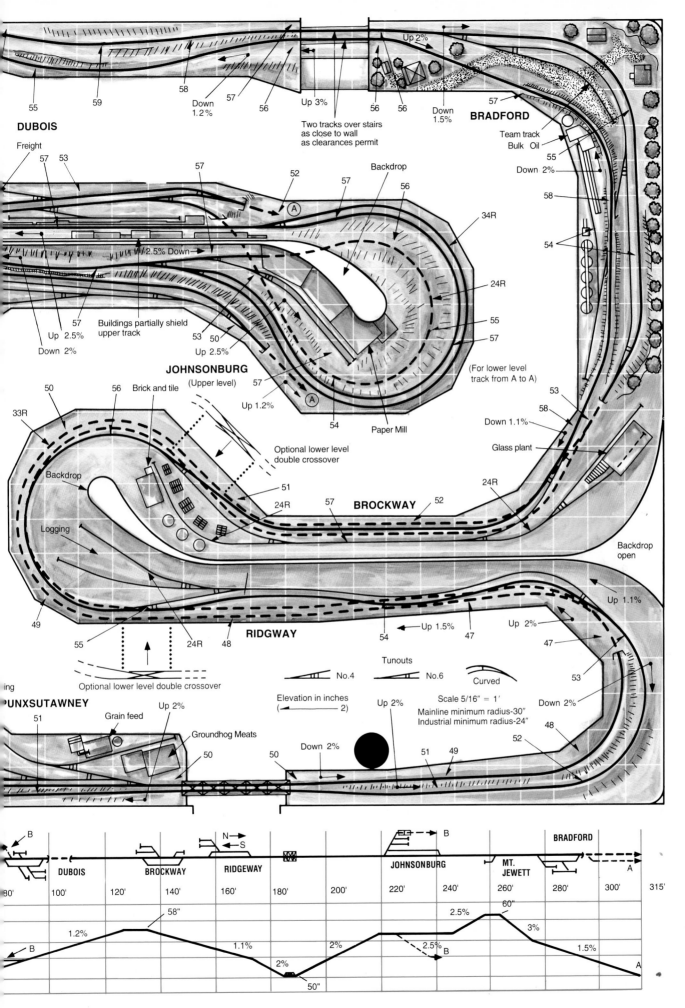

DUBOIS

Freight

55 · 59 · 58 · 57 · 56 · 55

Down 1.2%

Up 3%

Two tracks over stairs
as close to wall
as clearances permit

Up 2%

56 · 56 · Down 1.5% · 57 · **BRADFORD**

Team track
Bulk Oil

55

Down 2%

58

54

57 · 53 · 57 · 52 · 57 · 56

Backdrop

34R

24R

55

57

(For lower level
track from A to A)

2.5% Down →

A

Buildings partially shield
upper track

Up 2.5%

Down 2%

157

53 · 50

Up 2.5%

JOHNSONBURG
(Upper level)

57

Up 1.2%

A

54

Paper Mill

53

58

Down 1.1%

Glass plant

50 · 56 · Brick and tile

33R

Backdrop

Logging

49

55

24R · 48

RIDGWAY

51

24R

57 · **BROCKWAY** · 52

Optional lower level
double crossover

24R

Up 1.1%

Backdrop
open

Up 1.5%

54 · 47

Up 2%

47

53

Down 2%

Optional lower level double crossover

Tunouts

No.4 · No.6 · Curved

Elevation in inches
(————— 2)

Up 2%

Scale 5/16" = 1'
Mainline minimum radius-30"
Industrial minimum radius-24"

PUNXSUTAWNEY

51 · Grain feed · Up 2% · Groundhog Meats

50

50

Down 2%

51 · 49

52

48

Elevation profile (bottom):

B

N →
← S

B

BRADFORD

DUBOIS · **BROCKWAY** · **RIDGEWAY** · **JOHNSONBURG** · MT. JEWETT · A

80' · 100' · 120' · 140' · 160' · 180' · 200' · 220' · 240' · 260' · 280' · 300' · 315'

60"

58" · 2.5% · 3%

B · 1.2% · 1.1% · 2% · 2.5% B · 1.5% · A

2%

50"

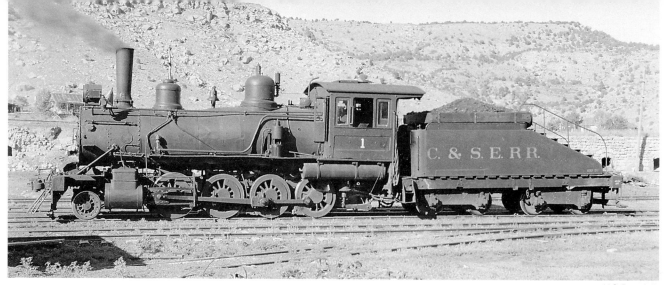

This standard gauge locomotive, the Colorado & South Eastern No. 1 2-8-0, worked the mountains of Colorado as far back as 1889, when it was Denver & Rio Grande No. 581.

M.C. Poor photo

EAGLE RIDGE

A western short line HO railroad with an interchange

Here's a layout designed for a modeler who knew exactly what he wanted:
• A western Colorado short line.
• An interchange with the Denver & Rio Grande Western.
• A scenic setting for his craftsman-type structures.
• On-layout car storage so he wouldn't have to handle his superdetailed rolling stock excessively.
• And to top it all, operating features ranging from hands-off running to individual car switching operations.

All of this had to fit in an irregularly shaped basement space, with a couple of support columns thrown in for good measure, but that actually turned out to be an advantage. The twists and turns allowed walkaround access from a center aisle, and the nooks and peninsulas served to break the layout up into separate scenes. The separation was enhanced by two peninsula backdrops raised to ceiling height. These backdrops were also used to conceal the support columns.

Model railroads tend to have more visible track than you'd see in similar prototype scenes. To create prototypical scenic vistas on the Eagle Ridge Ry., the track was limited to a minimum consistent with the operational objectives. Only the D&RGW is visible in the Falcon Flats area, and only the Eagle Ridge can be seen at Eagle Ridge and Cliffside. Both railroads meet at Crow River Jct., which is limited to a single interchange track along with passing sidings on each line.

The ERR does double back on itself in the Crow River Jct. area, but this is justified by considerable vertical separation. After all, this is a mountain railroad, and mountain railroads often have to double back on themselves to gain height.

REAR ACCESS

The D&RGW consists of a single-track line with a visible passing siding and hidden staging tracks. Preserving the scenic vistas meant hiding the staging tracks yet maintaining good access to them. The solution was a long access aisle hidden behind the scenery and backdrop. This aisle ranges in width from 30″ to only 18″, but additional maneuvering space is provided in the

---

Layout at a glance

Name: EAGLE RIDGE
Scale: HO
Space: 27' x 28' x 7' 6"
Location: Basement half
Operation: Short line and main line
Emphasis: Access to hidden staging

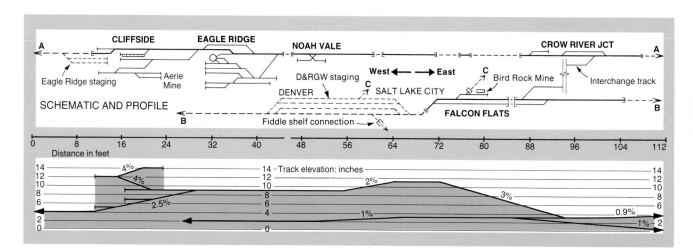

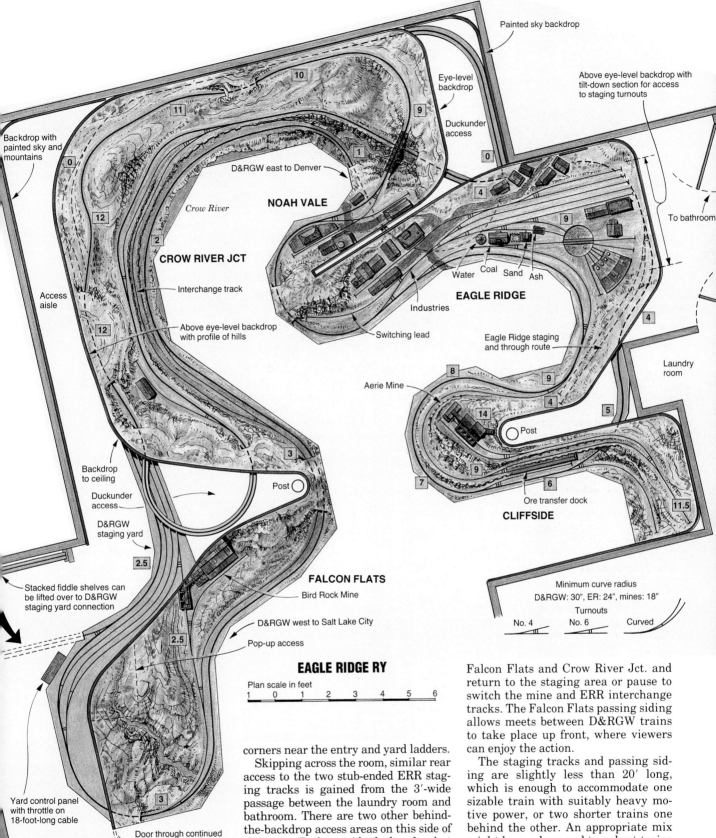

Painted sky backdrop

Eye-level backdrop

Duckunder access

Above eye-level backdrop with tilt-down section for access to staging turnouts

To bathroom

Laundry room

Backdrop with painted sky and mountains

D&RGW east to Denver

NOAH VALE

Crow River

CROW RIVER JCT

Interchange track

Above eye-level backdrop with profile of hills

Switching lead

Industries

Water Coal Sand Ash

EAGLE RIDGE

Eagle Ridge staging and through route

Access aisle

Aerie Mine

Post

Ore transfer dock

CLIFFSIDE

Backdrop to ceiling

Duckunder access

D&RGW staging yard

Post

Stacked fiddle shelves can be lifted over to D&RGW staging yard connection

FALCON FLATS

Bird Rock Mine

D&RGW west to Salt Lake City

Pop-up access

Minimum curve radius
D&RGW: 30″, ER: 24″, mines: 18″

Turnouts
No. 4   No. 6   Curved

EAGLE RIDGE RY

Plan scale in feet
1 0 1 2 3 4 5 6

Yard control panel with throttle on 18-foot-long cable

Coved corner and painted backdrop if door is not used

Door through continued backdrop (optional)

corners near the entry and yard ladders.

Skipping across the room, similar rear access to the two stub-ended ERR staging tracks is gained from the 3′-wide passage between the laundry room and bathroom. There are two other behind-the-backdrop access areas on this side of the room. Both provide duckunder, but stand-up, access to hidden trackage just in case anything goes wrong.

D&RGW OPERATION

The D&RGW is a continuous loop with enough additional features to allow realistic operation. D&RGW trains enter from the hidden staging tracks. They can then run nonstop through Falcon Flats and Crow River Jct. and return to the staging area or pause to switch the mine and ERR interchange tracks. The Falcon Flats passing siding allows meets between D&RGW trains to take place up front, where viewers can enjoy the action.

The staging tracks and passing siding are slightly less than 20′ long, which is enough to accommodate one sizable train with suitably heavy motive power, or two shorter trains one behind the other. An appropriate mix might be one long and two short trains headed in each direction. Then the staging tracks could hold all six trains out of sight, and there would be enough trains emerging at intervals to fill one operating session without repeat runs.

Two other features of the D&RGW are worth noting. The Bird Rock Mining tipple can be operated as an empties-in/loads-out interchange, but it also

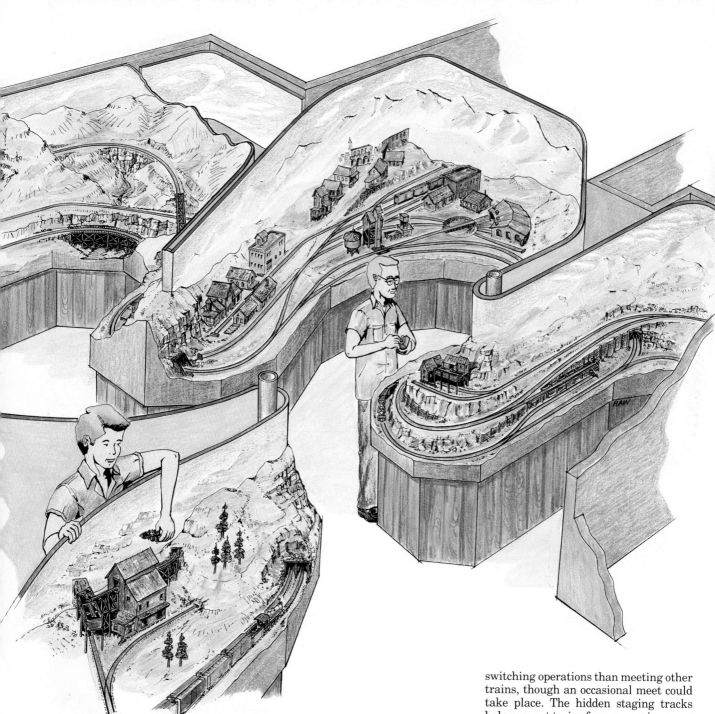

functions as a "hands-off-the-equipment" reversing track.

Remember that delicate, superdetailed equipment? On the wall behind the layout is a rack for shelves that can be used to take the equipment off the layout without touching it. On each shelf is a track that can be mated with the connecting track on the layout. The equipment can then be shoved out onto the shelf track, which can be lifted away and put on the storage rack. This way the cars need not be handled.

ERR OPERATION

The Eagle Ridge Ry. is also a continuous loop, but with a greater emphasis on switching. It connects with the D&RGW at Crow River Jct., then turns back on a 3 percent grade to climb toward Noah Vale and Eagle Ridge. In the other direction out of the junction, the ERR disappears under a truss bridge and runs past hidden staging tracks before reappearing at Cliffside.

The town of Eagle Ridge is the focal point of the short line. A yard, engine terminal, and industrial area make for lots of railroad action and visual interest. More industries are at Noah Vale, which is just that if cars aren't placed on the correct end of the locomotive before leaving Eagle Ridge. Setouts for Aerie Mine and Cliffside also have to be positioned on the correct end of the train by using the runaround at Eagle Ridge.

Trains on the ERR are short and infrequent. Passing sidings at Crow River Jct. and Eagle River are more for runaround switching operations than meeting other trains, though an occasional meet could take place. The hidden staging tracks help prevent trains from appearing more than once during an operating session.

TWO FOR THE SHOW

The layout's builder will want to display it for friends and family. The railroad needs to be animated at these times, but the host should be free to circulate and point out layout features. Switching or timetable operations are not appropriate for this sort of audience even if an operating crew could be assembled every time.

This is where the separate continuous loops of the D&RGW and the Eagle Ridge come into play. One train can be set running on each line without needing attention. The walkaround aisles provide freedom for the visitors and host to admire the scenes casually, like ancient gods surveying their domains. As a layout design, the ERR is human, the show, divine.

Ted Benson photo

A few renowned Western Pacific units congregate at Keddie on the morning of June 20, 1968. General Electric U30B No. 754 (left) waits in the hole with three other GEs and a GP35. The delivery of five U30Bs to the WP in late 1967 marked the first non-EMD power to enter road service on Western Pacific. F3A No. 803 (right) on the point of California Zephyr No. 17 was delivered in 1947 as one of the original CZ power units.

WESTERN PACIFIC

A 1000-square-foot N scale layout where scenery dwarfs the trains

An available layout space of almost 1,000 square feet may tempt many model railroaders to consider large scales, such as O and G. For that matter, the availability of a large layout space moves many to dream big: of big layouts, of big scenic views, of big trains in a prototype setting. Often, however, these dreams get chopped down in size, or in model railroading terms, scales. Such was the case with the Western Pacific RR.

The two most desired criteria on this nearly 1000-square-foot layout were big scenic views and a realistic prototype setting. O scale was the initial choice, but this scale makes modeling a setting in realistic proportion to its trains almost impossible. A football field would be needed for that. So scale preferences were scaled down and other sizes considered. S scale has more models

available than commonly believed, but its bulk was still too large for the desired effect. HO scale has by far the greatest number of products on the market, but the trains of 50 or so cars wanted to run on this layout would stretch nearly the entire length of one wall of the room. Z scale trains would readily fit along a wall and still be appropriately dwarfed by the scenery. Unfortunately, the variety of available Z scale models of American prototypes is not anywhere near what was needed.

That left N scale, which has much to recommend it. The size of the models fit well with the idea of running lots of trains in a prototype setting while retaining that sense of the scenery dwarfing the trains. A nice variety of good running equipment is available, so operation and availability presented no problems. The availability of a brass

model of the *California Zephyr* clinched the decision: N scale it was. The Western Pacific (WP) became a natural for the prototype. The *Zephyr* discovery had one other effect: It pinned down the modeling era to the years when first generation diesels were in their heyday.

THE LAYOUT DESIGN

The desire for big scenic vistas led to a layout designed as a walkalong configuration with relatively straight aisles. The realistic prototype setting desired required modeling such prominent features of the WP as the Feather River Canyon and the famed wye at Keddie, located about halfway up the canyon and forming the junction with the Northern Extension to the GN connection at Beiber.

Two problems cropped up when laying out Keddie. First, if patterned strictly af-

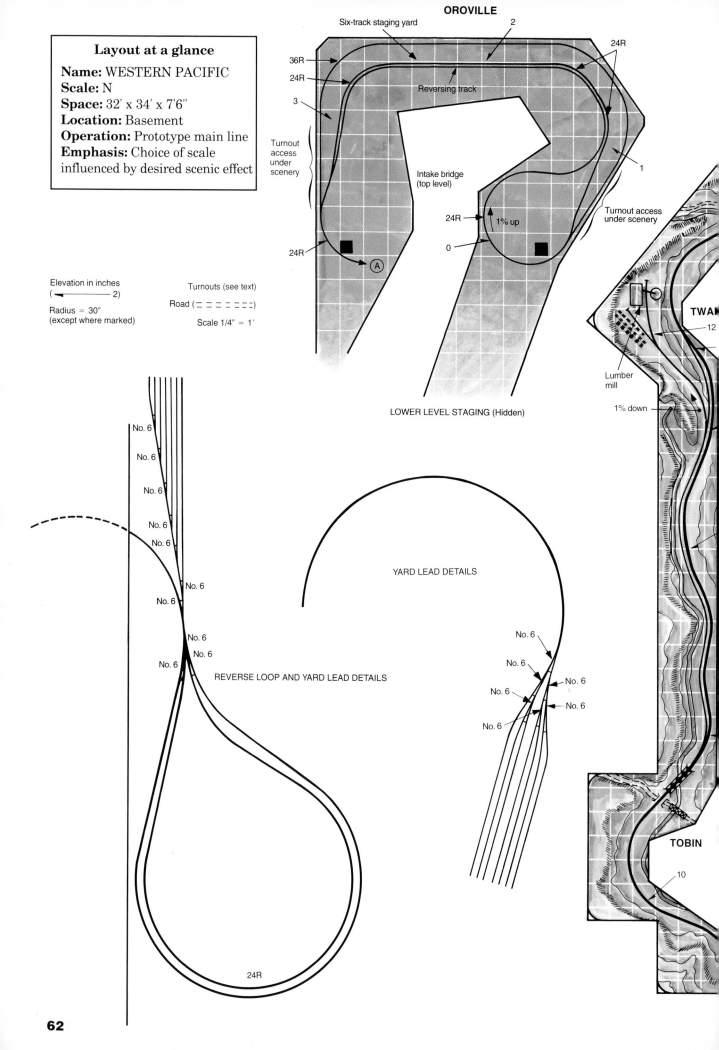

OROVILLE

Six-track staging yard

2

24R

36R

24R

Reversing track

3

24R

1

Turnout access under scenery

Intake bridge (top level)

24R

1% up

0

24R

Turnout access under scenery

A

Layout at a glance

Name: WESTERN PACIFIC
Scale: N
Space: 32' x 34' x 7'6"
Location: Basement
Operation: Prototype main line
Emphasis: Choice of scale influenced by desired scenic effect

Elevation in inches
(———— 2)

Radius = 30"
(except where marked)

Turnouts (see text)

Road (⌐ ⌐ ⌐ ⌐ ⌐ ⌐ ⌐)

Scale 1/4" = 1'

LOWER LEVEL STAGING (Hidden)

TWA

12

Lumber mill

1% down

No. 6
No. 6
No. 6
No. 6
No. 6
No. 6
No. 6
No. 6
No. 6
No. 6

YARD LEAD DETAILS

No. 6
No. 6
No. 6
No. 6
No. 6

REVERSE LOOP AND YARD LEAD DETAILS

No. 6
No. 6
No. 6

TOBIN

10

24R

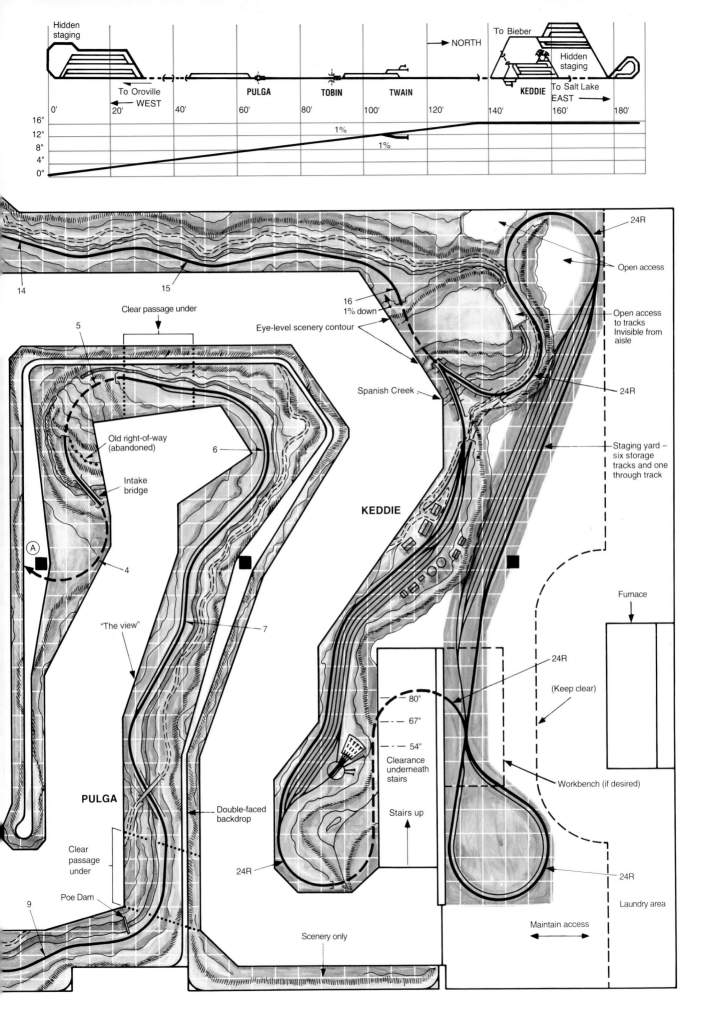

Hidden staging

To Bieber

Hidden staging

NORTH

KEDDIE

To Oroville
WEST

To Salt Lake
EAST

PULGA

TOBIN

TWAIN

0' 20' 40' 60' 80' 100' 120' 140' 160' 180'

16"
12"
8"
4"
0"

1%

1%

14

15

16
1% down

24R

Open access

Open access to tracks Invisible from aisle

24R

Clear passage under

5

Eye-level scenery contour

Spanish Creek

Old right-of-way (abandoned)

6

KEDDIE

Staging yard – six storage tracks and one through track

Intake bridge

A

4

Furnace

"The view"

7

PULGA

Double-faced backdrop

80"
67"
54"

24R

(Keep clear)

Clearance underneath stairs

Stairs up

Workbench (if desired)

Clear passage under

24R

24R

9

Poe Dam

Scenery only

Laundry area

Maintain access

ter the prototype, the track itself uses up a lot of space. Second, and even more difficult, the tracks at Keddie, as any wye, lead out in three directions. These problems were made even more difficult by the the walkalong configuration.

The solution was arrived at by using a combination of the design techniques already introduced. A stairway descending into the layout room helped fix the location of Keddie. The stairway and higher-than-eye-level scenery were used to separate a small section of the room from the main portion. Turnouts and other complicated trackage were kept within easy reach of the operating aisle. The leg of the wye connecting to the Northern extension was swung around away from the main aisle, but with sight lines carefully constructed to permit unseen open access from the rear of a large hill fronting on the aisle. Depending on the base height chosen for the layout, access to this track by reaching over the eye-level scenery or a backdrop might also be possible.

The staging tracks concealed behind the stairway represent both the Northern Extension to Bieber and the WP main line east to Salt Lake City. The reverse loop permits trains to be staged out of the yard in any direction, although a backing movement is required to return a train headed east in the yard toward Keddie, headed west. An exception was made for the *Zephyr,* which, like all WP passenger trains, ran only on the Oakland-Salt Lake City main line. The *Zephyr* is staged on the inner track of the reversing loop for easy return to Keddie. The illustrations on page 62 show the reversing loop and yard lead laid out with No. 6 turnouts.

Once Keddie was laid out, the remainder of the WP fell into place quickly. A hook-shaped peninsula with ceiling-high backdrops was used to divide the room into a series of long aisles with lengthy vistas.

A single-track line was run along the aisles, with long sidings added so that they wouldn't be visible from each other. This line made a series of almost constant curves to simulate the tortuous route forced on the prototype by the landscape of the Feather River canyon. The curves also add visual interest. Note how they're laid out — a series of constant radius arcs connected by short tangents rather than a series of wider curves of varying radius. Fewer calculations (or templates) are needed, making track construction easier on the model, just as on the prototype.

Note, too, that the 24″ and 30″ radii used for this N scale layout are consistent with HO scale practice. Increasing the curve radii by one scale, so to speak, enhances the feeling of real trains running in a prototype setting.

OTHER CONSIDERATIONS

The double-sided backdrops were also used to conceal the house support columns. Any resulting changes in air flow patterns can be simulated by hanging sheets from the ceiling in the backdrop locations. The existing vent system can be adjusted to test whether additional vents or exhaust ducts will be needed.

The single dead-end aisle pattern has the potential to bottleneck operators. Two locations have been designated as clear areas to provide duck-under short cuts for operating or maintenance crews. For visiting groups, the best rule would be to keep to the left, walking all the way in to the end of the aisle and then viewing the layout in detail while returning.

ENHANCING THE ILLUSIONS

Frank Ellison gained renown for his Delta Lines, one of the earliest private layouts to be scenicked and operated as a real railroad. Ellison was a newspaperman who had spent many years in the theater business. He wrote several articles on model railroading, many of which stressed the similarities between his favorite hobby and show business. Ellison believed that model railroaders could use theatrical set design techniques to create illusions, and that model railroad operation could be staged to create the illusion of theatrical drama.

The basis for creating such illusions on the model WP comes from a quick look at the prototype. The WP runs westward from Keddie down to Oroville, California, on a constant one percent grade through the spectacular canyon of the Feather River. The railroad runs close to the canyon floor, rising in relation to the floor only due to differences between the natural slope and the railroad grade. Power dams have added a stair-step relationship between the railroad and the water levels in several areas of the canyon.

Modeling the scenic vistas of the prototype in this area requires the trickery Ellison advocated. Two scenicking problems were faced. Extending the prototype scenery down to the floor would have put the railroad at an impractically low height. Conversely, putting the railroad at a more normal height would have resulted in a loss of that sense of viewing the canyon from the bottom up. To circumvent these problems we added a small shelf of scenery on the side of the aisle opposite the railroad to represent the "other" side of the canyon. Painting everything below the layout a dark color, coupled with adding overhead valances to shield the layout lighting, helps to cause the aisle to fade from the viewer's consciousness and enhance the illusion of the railroad being in the bottom of a canyon.

The plasterwork required to achieve all this will take time, even though much of this creation will be covered by trees. Obtaining the thousands of trees needed also will take time. A mass production effort of sorts is called for, using such basic tree-building materials as bumpy chenille and furnace filters.

Visual illusions are not the only ones. Hearing illusions can be used to create the overall effect of being in the Feather River canyon. You could play tapes containing sounds commonly heard in the forest, such as moving water and chirping birds, at low volume through strategically located speakers. The screech of

The Western Pacific's SWG, with F7A unit 913D on the point, leaves the main line and heads for the Fourth Subdivision over the north leg of the famous wye trestle at Keddie, California. No model of the Western Pacific would seem complete without this wye.

saws and other machinery at work would be particularly effective played through a speaker hidden in the lumber mill at Twain.

The mass of trees, while a problem to create, can also be used to tickle another illusion based on smell. Pine scent is readily available and could be applied to forested areas. It wouldn't take much ingenuity to rig up a contrivance to spray small quantities of the scent into the air as visitors passed a designated location.

It might even be possible to create the smell of burning wood emanating from the waste incinerator at the sawmill.

The illusion would not be complete without action, and it is the movement of trains that draws people along the aisles. The WP is almost completely a train running operation. The only spurs for setting out cars are located at the lumber mill and at Keddie. More switching activity is possible at Keddie, however, if some trains are stopped for cars

to be sorted between mainline and Northern Extension destinations.

Most of the trains are through runs between the hidden staging yards representing Bieber/Salt Lake and Oroville. Six staging tracks at both these locations, coupled with the Keddie yard and the Pulga and Tobin sidings, should hold enough trains for an operating session with few repetitions. Mix in night lighting to indicate a change of acts and the stage is set for great model railroading.

A busy moment on Southern Pacific's Tehachapi Loop. The double-headed San Joaquin Daylight is seen descending the loop around the central hill, headed for the tunnel. In the foreground a long freight, with a cab-ahead articulated road engine up front, is just getting under way on the passing track. On a third track, nearer the camera, stand the cars of a work train.

TEHACHAPI PASS

The ultimate walkaround layout

I'll bet most model railroaders dream about building, or at least being involved with, the ultimate model railroad. The Tehachapi Pass RR was such a dream, but it is one that is being made into reality by the La Mesa Model Railroad Club. La Mesa members Tony Andersen and Dave Willoughby started with prototype engineering drawings for the Southern Pacific/Atchison, Topeka & Santa Fe route between Bakersfield and Mojave and converted them into a breathtaking walkaround layout design.

The club occupies a 136′ x 60′ x 18′ space in the San Diego Model Railroad Museum. Within that space, Dave and Tony laid out public viewing aisles, engineers' walkaround aisles, and 25 scale miles of model railroad line.

Curves were maintained in prototype relation to each other to replicate the real scenic vistas. A 60 percent selective compression factor was used for essential trackage; that is 100-car prototype sidings were reduced to 60 cars on the model, and 10-degree curves, which would scale to 78″ radius, were reduced to 48″ radius — the layout minimum. Greater compression was used elsewhere, particularly where the track is hidden in tunnels or penetrates the backdrop to scale down the 75-mile length of the prototype route.

The 2.5 percent grade through the real Tehachapi Pass was reduced to 2.25 percent on the model so the track wouldn't climb through the ceiling. Even at that, one-third of the layout will be housed on a mezzanine, with

the track rising to about 13′ above the base of the building.

The decision to use a walkaround design was motivated by two factors. The club's previous layout was to some extent marred by poor access, leaving members determined to avoid similar problems this time around. Thus, it was agreed all operating trackage would be within easy reach. Where the walkaround aisles wouldn't meet this criteria because of scenic considerations, movable scenery sections and out-of-sight access ports were incorporated in the design. Duck-under access hatches were also included where it was necessary to reach remote sections of the scenery.

The second motivating factor was the desire to have realistic operation on a huge railroad. Real trains are run by

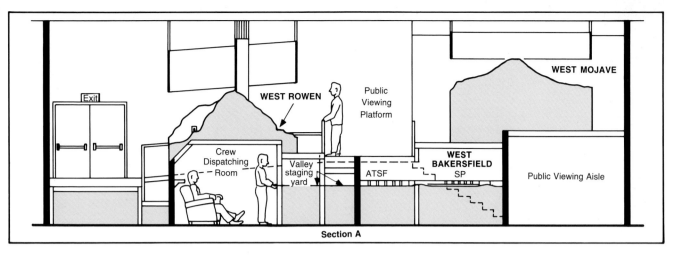

Section A

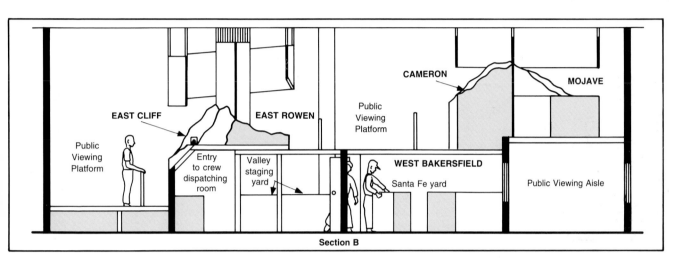

Section B

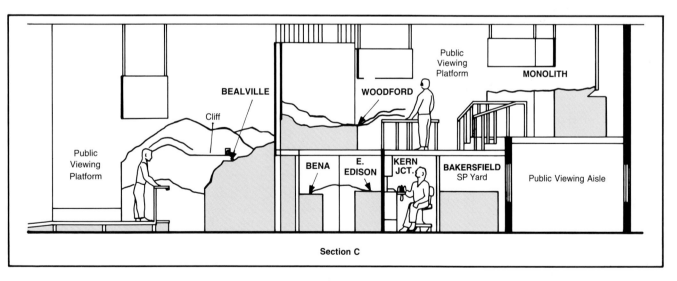

Section C

engineers, not by tower operators passing control of the trains along as they reach territorial boundaries. So, a single engineer was assigned control of one train from start to finish of its run. The sheer size of the layout precluded a single central operating location for the engineers, making walkaround control the only feasible method of operation.

NON-RAILROAD DESIGN FACTORS

Tehachapi Pass is one of four permanent model railroad layouts in the San Diego Model Railroad Museum. The museum is located in the Casa de Balboa, a city building in San Diego's Balboa Park. Designing layouts for public exhibition in public places requires grapling with some unusual problems. Construction materials and methods, lighting, ventilation, fire protection, public aisle widths, and handicapped access, to name a few, have to meet applicable codes. Few model railroads ever reach this point, but,

as the creators of the Tehachapi Pass can attest, when they do, advice from an architect is a must.

The regular public display of layouts imposes operational constraints, too. To get trains running and ready for public display as early as possible, phased construction has to be employed. The Tehachapi Pass was no exception: The first phase of its construction was the 30′ x 80′ section between Tunnel 1/2 and Cliff, encompassing the horseshoe curve at Caliente.

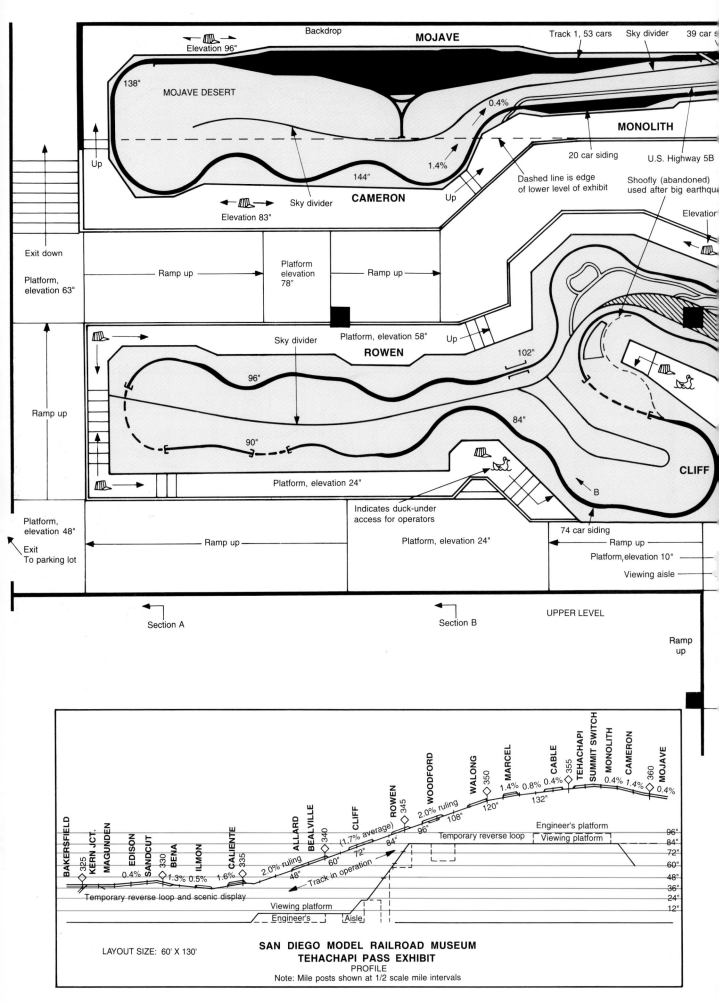

SAN DIEGO MODEL RAILROAD MUSEUM
TEHACHAPI PASS EXHIBIT
PROFILE
Note: Mile posts shown at 1/2 scale mile intervals

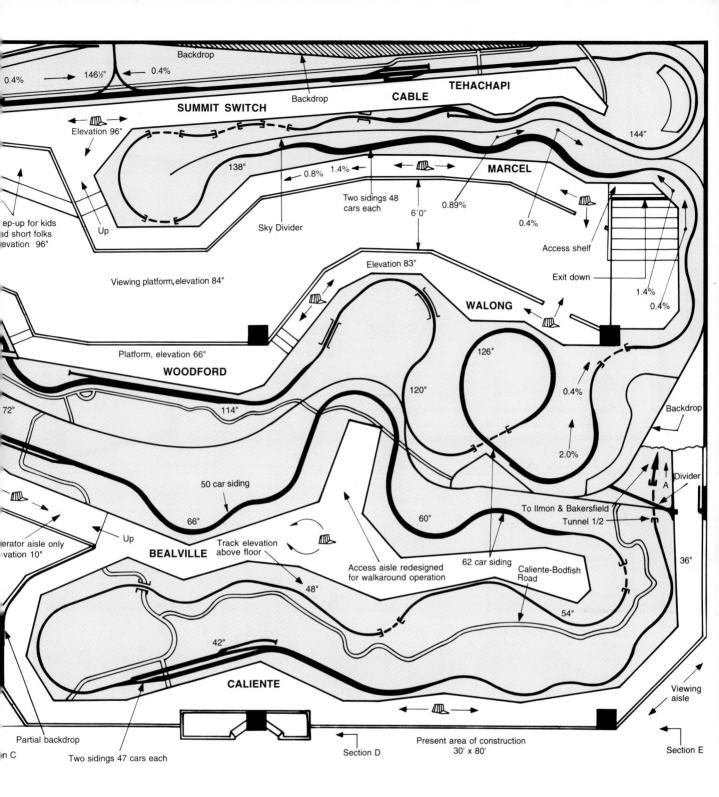

Backdrop — Backdrop — CABLE — TEHACHAPI
146½" — 0.4% — 0.4%
SUMMIT SWITCH
Elevation 96"
138"
0.8% — 1.4% — MARCEL
Two sidings 48 cars each
0.89% — 0.4%
6'0"
Sky Divider
144"
Access shelf
Exit down
1.4%
0.4%
ep-up for kids nd short folks evation 96"
Up
Viewing platform, elevation 84"
Elevation 83"
WALONG
126"
120"
0.4%
Platform, elevation 66"
WOODFORD
114"
Backdrop
72"
2.0%
A
50 car siding
To Ilmon & Bakersfield
Tunnel 1/2
Divider
erator aisle only vation 10"
Up
66"
60"
62 car siding
Caliente-Bodfish Road
36"
BEALVILLE
Track elevation above floor
48"
Access aisle redesigned for walkaround operation
54"
42"
CALIENTE
Viewing aisle
Partial backdrop
n C
Two sidings 47 cars each
Section D
Present area of construction 30' x 80'
Section E

Temporary reversing loops at each end of the permanent track permitted continuous train operation. These loop areas were later expanded to include staging tracks for more than 1000 cars and locomotives.

The regular operation of layouts on public display also imposes requirements on the control system. To minimize the need for operators, the layout has to be capable of being run by one person. This is easily achieved: Multiposition throttle selector switches for each block can be lined up so that one throttle is connected to all blocks for such operation. The Tehachapi Pass has made provisions for future automation as the layout grows large enough to make this necessary during the public operation hours.

For normal walkaround operation, the engineers line the selector switches to connect their particular throttle to the blocks as they pass the control panels. This allows the railroad to accommodate a large number of operators during timetable operating sessions.

Most model railroaders will never be associated with a huge layout like Tehachapi Pass, but it is built using the same walkaround design principles that apply to small layouts.

Layout at a glance

Name: TEHACHAPI PASS
Scale: HO
Space: 136' x 60' x 18'
Location: San Diego Model Railroad Museum
Operation: Mountain main line with prototypic length trains
Emphasis: Daily public operation

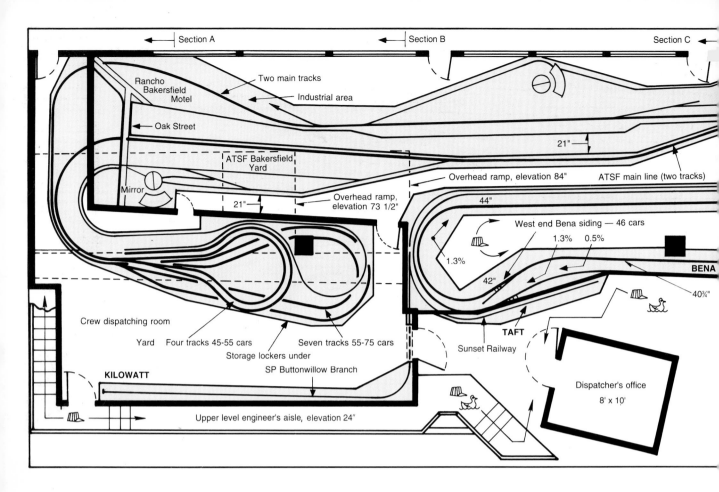

Section A ←   Section B ←   Section C ←

Rancho Bakersfield Motel

Two main tracks

Industrial area

Oak Street

ATSF Bakersfield Yard

21"

Mirror

21"

Overhead ramp, elevation 73 1/2"

Overhead ramp, elevation 84"

ATSF main line (two tracks)

44"

West end Bena siding — 46 cars

1.3%   0.5%

1.3%

42"

BENA

40¾"

Crew dispatching room

Yard   Four tracks 45-55 cars

Storage lockers under

SP Buttonwillow Branch

Seven tracks 55-75 cars

TAFT

Sunset Railway

Dispatcher's office
8' x 10'

KILOWATT

Upper level engineer's aisle, elevation 24"

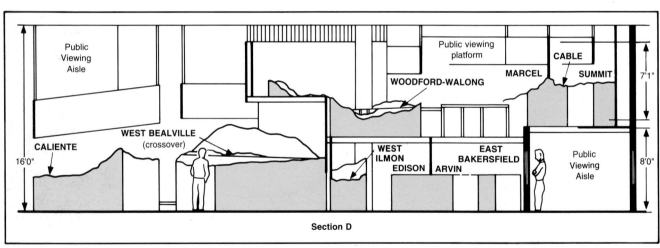

Public Viewing Aisle

Public viewing platform

CABLE

MARCEL   SUMMIT

WOODFORD-WALONG

7'1"

WEST BEALVILLE
(crossover)

CALIENTE

WEST
ILMON
EDISON
ARVIN

EAST
BAKERSFIELD

Public Viewing Aisle

16'0"

8'0"

Section D

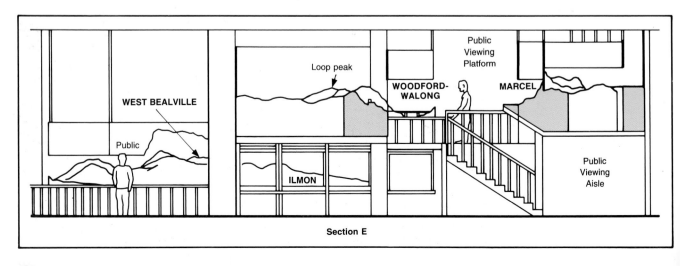

Loop peak

Public Viewing Platform

WEST BEALVILLE

WOODFORD-WALONG

MARCEL

Public

ILMON

Public Viewing Aisle

Section E

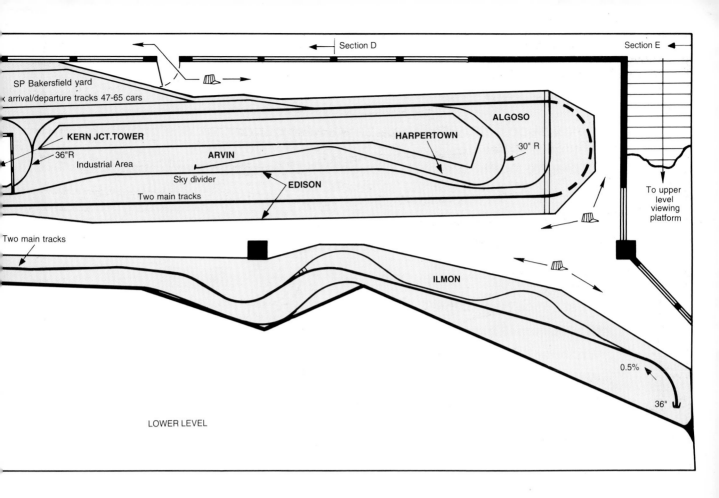

Section D

Section E

SP Bakersfield yard

arrival/departure tracks 47-65 cars

ALGOSO

KERN JCT. TOWER

HARPERTOWN

36"R

ARVIN

30" R

Industrial Area

Sky divider

EDISON

Two main tracks

To upper
level
viewing
platform

Two main tracks

ILMON

0.5%

36"

LOWER LEVEL

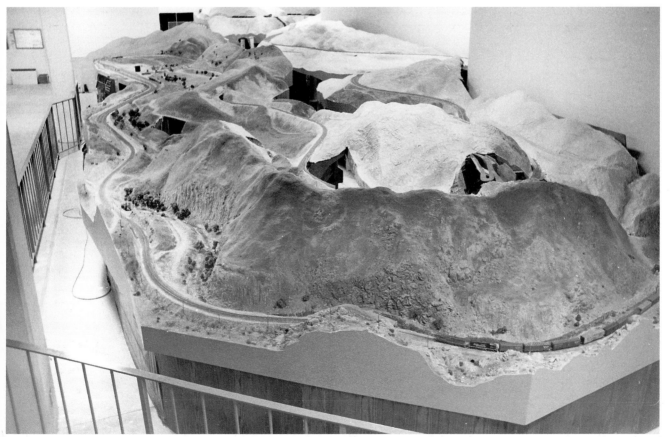

Walkaround design can be applied to any size railroad. The La Mesa Model Railroad Club's model of Tehachapi Pass includes public viewing aisles (outside the fence), walkaround operating aisles (between the fence and layout and in the center of the layout), and access hatches (left to right in middle of photo) for working on the scenery. The train barely discernable at Cliff (top center of photo) is 70′ and eight scale track miles from the train (foreground) exiting tunnel.

WALKAROUND DESIGN CHECKLIST

I hope this book convinces you that walkaround track designs offer many advantages over other designs. Yes, you can run into some challenging problems, but they're nothing a little thought or imagination can't overcome. The track plans in this book illustrate as much. They also show that thinking ahead can save you lots of hassle later on. So here's a list of questions you should consider before designing a walkaround layout (a discussion of each question is found in the chapter(s) referenced):

- [ ] What space is available for my layout? (Union Pacific)
- [ ] How tall am I? (Introduction and Carson & Colorado)
- [ ] What track standards will I use? (Omaha & North Western)
- [ ] Will I have to move my layout frequently? (Bekin United RR)
- [ ] How much railroad do I want? (Angels Branch and Allentown Western)
- [ ] What type of equipment do I want to run? (Union Pacific and Angels Branch)
- [ ] Will my layout emphasize scenery? (Shenango Valley and Western Pacific)
- [ ] Do I want car-switching operations? (Oakville Central and Bekin United RR)
- [ ] Do I want to feature continuous running? (Raton Pass and Anon & Muss)
- [ ] If I'm building a larger layout, have I considered alternatives? (Mahoning Creek)
- [ ] Should I include staging tracks? (Allentown Western and Eagle Ridge)
- [ ] Do I want to model a prototype? (Angels Branch, Carson & Colorado, Reader Railroad, and Tehachapi Pass)
- [ ] Are my aisles wide enough for the operating crew and visitors? (Anon & Muss)
- [ ] Can the construction of my layout be accomplished in phases compatible with operation? (Anon & Muss and Omaha & North Western)
- [ ] What type of controls will I use? (Raton Pass, Omaha & North Western, Mahoning Creek, and Tehachapi Pass)
- [ ] And, finally, does my plan meet the first three rules of layout design? (1) access (for construction), (2) access (for operation), and (3) access (for maintenance)

To Marge
Who made it all possible